FACE
READING

FACE READING

Secrets of the Chinese Masters

Simon Brown

STERLING

New York / London
www.sterlingpublishing.com

Library of Congress Cataloging-in-Publication
Data Available

2   4   6   8   10   9   7   5   3   1

Published in 2008 by Sterling Publishing Co., Inc.
387 Park Avenue South, New York, NY 10016

First published in Great Britain in 2007 by Godsfield
Press, a division of Octopus Publishing Group Ltd
2-4 Heron Quays, London E14 4JP, UK

Distributed in Canada by Sterling Publishing
$^{C}/_{O}$ Canadian Manda Group. 165 Dufferin Street
Toronto, Ontario, Canada M6K 3H6

For information about custom editions, special sales,
premium and corporate purchases, please contact
Sterling Special Sales Department at 800-805-5489 or
specialsales@sterlingpub.com.

Manufactured in China
All Rights Reserved

Sterling ISBN-13: 978-1-4027-5982-6
Sterling ISBN-10: 1-4027-5982-7

Simon Brown asserts the moral right to be identified
as the author of this work

Contents

Chapter 1

PRINCIPLES OF FACE READING

The following pages will introduce you to face reading, how it started and how it works. Hopefully, it will provide the information to further your understanding of this ancient skill and give your practice of face reading a strong foundation. Key to understanding face reading is to learn how the five elements connect us to the rhythms of nature and how each element is revealed in our physical and emotional bodies as well as on our faces.

What is face reading?

Essentially, face reading is the art of divining something about a person's character or health simply by looking at his or her face. We all face read and have done so since we were born. We have stored in our memory banks a library of faces and characters all matched up. Initially this was an essential tool to help protect us from potential predators but later we naturally developed it into a powerful tool to help us in all kinds of social interactions.

Much of this facial analysis happens subconsciously. You could be introduced to someone at a party and your mind might notice that his mouth is similar to another man that you know. Without realizing it you will instinctively make initial assumptions about this person based on your previous experiences of the man with a similar mouth.

The reason we choose to do this with faces is that they are the most exposed part of our bodies and the most revealing. Not only does the face have five distinct features – its shape, eyebrows, eyes, nose and mouth – but two of these, the eyes and mouth, are highly mobile features giving out a huge amount of information about the person behind the face. In addition, the cheeks change colour according to the immediate emotions in a pale-skinned person.

The art of face reading takes something we do intuitively and brings what we know up to our conscious mind so we can read faces with some consistency whenever we want. This could be applied to character readings or to gain an insight into our own or other people's states of health.

Face reading is a powerful tool and needs to be used wisely, with respect for other people's feelings and with an understanding of the implications of applying it.

The memorable features in this face are small eyes and a wide smile.

A code of ethics for face reading

1 Do not make comments based on a face reading unless asked to.

2 Do not pass on the information that you discover during a face-reading session to another person without permission from your subject.

3 Focus on the person's positive attributes unless asked to solve a particular problem. In most situations people do not want to hear about their weaknesses or be criticized. This may not be healthy for their self-esteem and confidence. The exception to this rule would be if someone asks for help with a problem, such as in a relationship issue, and he or she wants to change things about him or herself to improve the situation.

4 Accept that face reading does not cover every aspect of someone's character and accept contrary opinions to your reading. If you feel that your subject is being honest, rather than defensive, then there is often much to learn from feedback to your face-reading comments.

5 Do not interpret someone's features as good or bad. Try to see character traits as different shades of grey rather than black or white.

6 Learn not to make lasting judgements based on face reading that may prejudice you or other people against someone. Use it to emphasize the positive aspects of someone and the ways in which you can interact most successfully with him or her. Always keep an open mind and measure your initial face reading against your long-term real-life experiences with someone.

7 When using face reading, compare like with like. Face reading is not designed to make comparisons between people of different ethnic origins, nor can it be used to make judgements about different groups of people who have similar facial features. One of the skills of face reading is to recognize how to observe when someone's face can provide important clues to his or her character and to be able to do this equally with people around the globe. For this reason, you will find that face reading is easiest in cultures with which you are familiar.

This man exhibits features that are naturally different according to his cultural heritage.

How does it work?

On one level face reading is simply interpreting the expression of a person's current emotional state. Our faces are highly reactive and therefore change according to the shift of emotions. A frown, raised eyebrows, the rate at which someone blinks, eye movement, a narrowing of the eyes, flushed cheeks, pursed lips or a clenched jaw are responses to internal feelings and send out an unspoken message. It might be that over a long period of time these expressions become ingrained in our faces.

Reading the character in the face

However, face reading goes further and the essential idea is that the emotional character with which we were born will also be reflected in the face with which we were born. Someone who has an innately outgoing, expressive character will also naturally have an outgoing, expressive face.

Of course, life changes our character and we learn to adjust our behaviour in different ways and these changes may not necessarily show up in a face reading. This is one instance where we need to be open and flexible in our readings.

We also learn how to use our faces to communicate. For example, we can consciously change our expression to make a point. Practically, face reading is done with the face in a relaxed state.

Emotional energy filters out through the skin leaving marks and signs that we use in face reading.

Oriental practice

The style of face reading described in this book originated in China and was developed in surrounding countries, such as Japan. In these countries there is a long history of combining emotions with physical bodies. There is no separation in Oriental thinking between physical and emotional health. More than this, Eastern cultures traditionally embraced the idea that we have subtle currents of electro-magnetic energy flowing through our bodies as part of their healing practices. This is called *chi* in China, *ki* in Japan and *prana* in India.

Our chi also extends beyond the human skin and will typically form a field 10–100 cm (4–39 inches) around a person and can now be photographed by a process called Kirlian photography. Chi is thought to carry people's emotions around their bodies so that every cell is fed with their blood, oxygen and chi. Chi in a person primarily carries thoughts, beliefs and emotions.

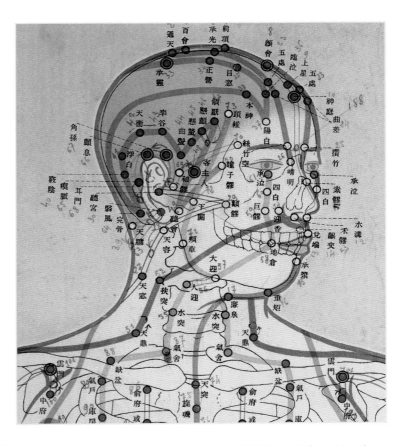

This drawing shows the paths of chi flow and the points where it can be most easily influenced.

As chi moves through the body it takes on different forms. The Chinese defined five of these forms and named them after five natural elements. As a person's chi moves through the body it filters up through the skin leaving its mark. Over time this will become a noticeable feature, something we can read on someone's face. At the same time chi flows according to physical constraints, a bit like water through its terrain, and in that sense our bone structure, posture, facial features and shape will influence the way chi flows and therefore what kinds of emotions and characteristics come most naturally to us.

In Oriental medicine emotions can be linked to physical states. So in the five-element theory a face reading can be used to understand the flow of chi in terms of the five elements and this in turn is related to the potential internal physical condition of a patient.

Over thousands of years, Oriental practitioners have built up a map of how chi and the emotions associated with it would affect different parts of the body and how this would show up on a person's face.

The history of face reading

Traditional Chinese medicine was (and is) largely preventative. The aim was to try and predict the onset of a health problem long before it became serious and traditional practitioners based their reputation on how long their patients lived and how rarely they became ill.

Several techniques were developed to diagnose the early onset of an illness and some are still used today in treatments such as acupuncture and herbal medicine. Most common were face reading, pulse diagnosis, tongue diagnosis, acupressure point diagnosis, palmistry and observation of the patient's posture and behaviour.

Historically, face reading looked at each feature and compared it in terms of their position on the face, their size, prominence and, where applicable, the underlying bone structure and colour or texture of the skin. Each part of the face related to a particular organ and the emotions associated with that organ.

Five-element theory

One of the early theoretical models used was the five-element theory. It is probable that the five elements began as part of a farmer's almanac where each element relates to a different season. In addition, the months and days were described in terms of these elements. The elements would then help farmers know when to seed, plant and harvest.

In time these elements were applied to people, their characters and health. So someone might be seen as having more springtime, sunrise, wood energy and have more of the personality associated with the atmosphere at that time of year and day. Similarly,

Huang Ti is credited with writing the Yellow Emperor's Classic of Internal Medicine, *an original text on Chinese medicine.*

a person with too much hot summer, mid-day, fire energy might easily get stressed and find it harder to feel calm. Eventually this might contribute to heart problems.

Early history

The first written work on Chinese medicine is thought to have been by Huang Ti and titled the *Yellow Emperor's Classic of Internal Medicine*, which is dated to approximately 260 BCE to 220 CE. These texts show that medical practitioners had already developed an in-depth knowledge of chi energy, yin and yang and the five elements. In addition, various forms of diagnosis were employed using the outer part of the body to read what was happening inside.

During the Confucian period around 550 BCE face reading became popular throughout China, spreading to the nearby countries of Japan, India and Korea.

Western interpretations

Face reading also became popular in Europe under the label of physiognomy. In 1272 Michael Scott wrote his book *De Hominis Physiognomia* on the subject; and more recently during the late 18th century, the Swiss pastor Johann Lavater (1741–1801) wrote his opus *Physiognomische Fragmente zur Beförderung der Menschenkenntnis und Menschenliebe* on the art of face reading.

Japanese theories

Meanwhile in Japan Nanboku Mizuno became famous for his impressive skills in physiognomy. He was born about 1750 and later wrote an influential book called *Food Governs Destiny*. More recently, during the early 20th century, George Ohsawa, inspired by Dr Ishizuka, who specialized in food and healing, founded a

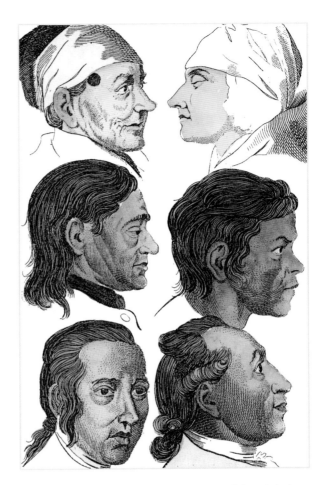

Early face reading looked for the appearance of the criminal mind and many studies were made of skulls and living faces.

movement called macrobiotics. The central philosophy is that you can change your health through your diet. Face reading was used to assess which diet would be most successful for an individual.

During the 1970s Michio Kushi, one of George Ohsawa's students, refined and developed his impressive face-reading skills to the point that thousands of people have sought his advice from all over the world.

Observation

Face reading is all about being able to distinguish subtle differences from one face to another and to notice changes from day to day in your own or other people's faces. To learn how to face read you will need to be able to make comparisons and get used to looking at different facial features.

This can take years of practice. I started by sitting in places where I would be able to observe hundreds of people. Train stations, markets, cafés, airports or busy streets are all examples. Michio Kushi recommended that I take just one feature at a time, so I would spend an hour looking at noses, then an hour looking at mouths and so on. As time went by I was able to differentiate between different face shapes, skin colorations, full or thin lips, large or small eyes until I had a good feel for all the features on the face.

The more skilful your observational skills the more accurate your reading will be so take the time to get used to looking at as many live faces as possible. Initially, you will find it best to see faces in consistent conditions and for this reason I recommend you begin looking at faces in natural light. Different kinds of lighting will change the appearance of a face and this can be confusing.

At this stage there is no need to try to read a face or make any kind of analysis, just look for some of the distinctive feature in the box opposite.

Here the subject's upper lip appears thin, her chin prominent and her left eyebrow slopes upwards.

WHAT TO LOOK FOR

Face Is it round, oval or square-shaped? Try covering up the ears and ignoring the hair to help you get a consistent reading.

Forehead Is it tall or short? Does the forehead slope back in profile? Can you see lines across the forehead? Are there spots across the forehead or around the temples?

Eyebrows Do they arch? Are they full and bushy? How long are they? Do they drop at the outer ends?

Eyes Are they large or small? Are they spaced closely together or apart? Is the eye movement fast and erratic or steady? How often does the person blink?

Nose Is it bulbous or pinched? Large or small? Does it have a red or purple hue? Is it shiny?

Cheeks Are they full or sunken? A rosy colour or sallow? Do they appear to flush easily? Can you see the cheekbone?

Ears Large or small? Is the upper, middle or lower part most developed? Are the ears higher or lower on the face? Is the earlobe detached? Does the earlobe have a line across it?

Lines between nose and upper lip Is the groove between the lines deep? Are the lines long? Do they produce a strong curve in the upper lip?

Chin Is it spotty? Does it have a dimple? Is it indented? Does it look greasy?

Jaw Is it well defined? Does the chin jut forward? Is the jaw broad, forming the widest part of the face?

This man has a tall, oval face shape, small narrow eyes and a strong chin.

Mouth Are the lips full or thin? Does the mouth open more vertically or horizontally? Are the lips red, purple or pale? Can you see little lines around the lips?

Intuition

Face reading relies on an element of intuition. This is where you will draw on the experience of all the faces and characters you have matched up in your head along with the face-reading secrets in this book to make a complete reading.

To be able to face read effectively you will need to be able to take a wide range of information from a face and turn it into a meaningful reading. Some of the information may be contradictory and the skill of the reader is in being able to use the most important characteristics to draw conclusions.

Study this book carefully and apply each face-reading secret to as many faces as possible. Try to master one feature at a time before moving on. At the same time avoid being over-analytical. The most successful strategy is to study face reading with an open mind and soak up the information naturally through practice rather than being overly conceptual. Try not to get stuck interpreting a lot of different bits of information.

Daily practice

A good exercise when in public places is to observe individuals and see which feature stands out most on his or her face. Make a mental note of which of the five element energies this feature reminds you of, then connect this with other observations you can make. For example, observe the person's choice of clothing, posture, behaviour, the newspaper or magazine he or she reads, or the way that person moves. There is no need to read anything into your observations – it is simply a way to add to your internal database and this in time will help you better use your intuition when face reading.

Another way to increase your experience of face reading is to go the internet and read about people's histories. Look at the person's face and match aspects of the face with what he or she did in life.

Learning to read

Once you have read through this book and practised every aspect of face reading, you will be ready to try a complete reading. Begin by closing your

To practice face reading, look for a face in a crowd and make a mental note of the way he walks, the clothes he wears and his expression.

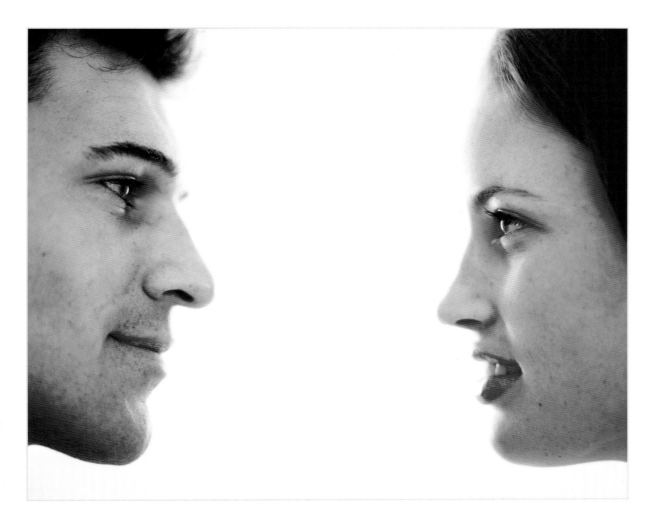

eyes, taking a few slow, deep breaths and just focus on the feeling of breathing to empty your mind.

When you are ready, open your eyes slowly and look at the person's face. At this point just continue to meditate on your breathing. See the face and remain completely relaxed. In this moment you may find that various intuitive thoughts come into your head.

Make a mental note of each thought and when this process runs dry, start to look at the face in a more reasoned manner. Look for the features that make the

Initially you might feel a little uncomfortable looking into someone's face. Practice on friends and family members until you can just relax.

biggest impression and use this to help decide the balance of the energies of the five elements.

Finally start looking at the detail of each feature to see what more you can learn about the person. This practice will help you refine your original observations and perhaps add interesting details.

Five-element theory

The five-element theory is based on an ancient Chinese calendar where five types of energies were assigned to different days, months and years. This was orientated around the equinoxes and solstices to help farmers plan ahead and organize their agricultural cycles.

The correspondence between human relationships and the cycles of the days, seasons and Moon were well recognized among traditional Chinese healers and the five-element theory became a fundamental part of traditional healing.

This theory is an insightful description of five types of energy, as we can experience each energy by going out into nature at the appropriate time of day and season. The important thing to remember is that the names – wood, fire, earth, metal and water – are simply names and not the energy itself. For example, metal energy is similar to the feeling you might have when watching the sun set in the autumn and not the metal itself.

If we stay with the five elements in terms of agriculture then the elements follow on from each other in the following order:

• **Wood** – spring
• **Fire** – summer
• **Earth** – late summer
• **Metal** – autumn
• **Water –** winter

Then the cycle repeats itself all over again. This is considered a harmonious reflection of nature. However, if one of the elements or seasons is weak then the following element or phase of a growing cycle will be disturbed.

Five elements and the face

When read in the face, the five elements can provide clues to the type of energy within the person behind the face. For example, someone with a fire complexion will have a more fiery, mid-day, summer energy inside, while another person might have sunken cheeks that signify metal energy and he or she may have more of the energy of the sunset and autumn. In terms of this book, the main aim is to be able to identify which elements are strongest in a person and then to use this to better understand what is happening within the individual.

In Chinese medicine, each element is associated with a pair of organs and different kinds of emotions, and a diagnosis that indicates an excess of the energy of one element and a deficiency in another will suggest that there are imbalances in terms of emotions and the internal functions of the body.

Each element is associated with a direction, reflecting the way that particular energy tends to flow. This is an essential aspect of the theory as it helps us see the five elements in a person. So if, for example, someone appears as though his or her energy moves up the body strongly then we can assume he or she has more wood, sunrise, spring energy. By feeling that sunrise, spring atmosphere in nature we can better understand the feelings inside that person.

THE FIVE ELEMENTS AND THEIR ATTRIBUTES

Element	Time of day	Season	Direction	Organs	Key Emotion
Wood	Sunrise	Spring	Upwards	Liver and gallbladder	Anger, assertive, activity, positive attitude, enthusiasm
Fire	Mid-day	Summer	Outwards	Heart and small intestine	Hysteria, excitement, expressive, outgoing, social
Earth	Afternoon	Late summer	Downwards	Spleen, pancreas and stomach	Jealousy, quality of life, practicality, stability, homely
Metal	Evening	Autumn	Inwards	Lungs and colon	Depression, playfulness, contentment, contained, inner strength
Water	Night	Winter	Flowing in any direction	Kidney and bladder	Fear, objective, artistic, original, flexibility

Character and health of each element

Following is a brief description of the character and health for each element and will be an essential guide for interpreting your readings. Each of us has all the elements present within us, although some may be more dominant than others; we are, therefore, looking at subtle increases of one energy over another.

Wood

This is the element of sunrise and springtime, whose energy is up, fresh and new. This is an energy that has the feel of new growth and the beginning of the day. In nature this is a time of new buds and rising vitality. Imagine walking barefoot through a park as the sun comes up over the horizon in the spring, feeling the dew rise up off the grass and nature waking up around you – this is the feeling of wood chi.

Character Wood energy encourages enthusiasm, a desire to start new projects and to feel ambitious. This springtime feeling helps you want to be busy, active and get on with life. In excess, it can risk making the person impatient, angry and aggressive. It is a good energy for being focused and getting on with the job in hand but can lead to narrow-mindedness and difficulty in listening to others' opinions.

When deficient in a person, it can risk making the person lack the desire to move forwards in life, lack self-esteem and feel dull.

Health An excess of wood chi can lead to energy moving up the body too quickly. This energy relates to the liver and in excess could encourage an enlarged liver and over-activity.

Rising eyebrows and a tall face suggest this woman has wood energy that would help her to be assertive.

A broad open face with full cheeks, shiny eyes and expressive features suggests a wealth of fire energy.

A deficiency of wood chi risks poor liver function, difficulty in digesting fats and blood disorders.

Fire

This is the element of mid-day and summer, with energy that is hot, expansive and radiant. This energy has the bright, shimmering chi of summer. In nature flowers are in full bloom attracting bees. Imagine being out in nature in the middle of a summer's day with the full sun and the bright colours of wild flowers in bloom.

Character This energy encourages expression, a flamboyant nature and a colourful appearance. It is a chi that is mentally stimulating and increases the desire to express emotions. This is a helpful energy when you want to live in the moment.

In excess, this energy risks over-excitement, hysteria and self-obsession. It is an excellent chi for being noticed, attracting attention and being entertaining but a person with too much fire chi can be easily led by the emotions of the moment and seem to only do what he or she feels like at the time.

If deficient in this element, the person can feel flat, lack spontaneity and feel less passion.

Health In excess, fire chi can increase feelings of stress and lead to high blood pressure, eventually risking heart problems. Bringing energy out to the periphery too quickly can exacerbate skin rashes, eczema and swellings.

In deficiency, fire chi risks poor circulation and a dull superficial appearance.

Earth

The element of afternoon and late summer energy is settling, downwards and slower. In nature the fruit is ripening on the vine rather than growing – nature is taking what it has and improving upon it. Imagine walking through fields in the afternoon when the leaves are starting to turn brown and the fruit is ready for picking.

Character Earth chi energy encourages a practical, methodical nature that emphasizes quality of life. This settling energy is ideal for deepening long-term relationships and finding ways to make the most of what you have.

In excess, it can lead to feeling stuck and unable to experiment or seek out broader horizons or take on challenges. It is helpful for feeling homely, cosy and secure but could lead to feeling too cautious.

In deficiency, a person might be rash as well as inconsiderate and irresponsible.

Health In excess, this chi can increase appetite and the risk of binge eating. It could also lead to instable blood sugar levels and in the long term to diabetes.

In deficiency, a person might experience poor digestion, slow immune system response and be prone to digestive infections.

Metal

The element of sunset and autumn energy is inward, central and concentrated. This end-of-the-day, harvest energy is ideal for a sense of completion and reaping the rewards of your hard work. Imagine sitting on a beach watching the sun go down over the horizon.

Character In terms of character, metal chi builds up inner strength, dignity and a feeling of being self - contained. The inward nature of metal chi and its ability to draw energy in also increases the ability to acquire material wealth but suggests an ability to draw people into your world.

In excess, this energy could lead someone to feel withdrawn, depressed and melancholic. It is an energy that helps you be tenacious and persistent at working through challenges but can also result in holding on to things for too long.

When this chi is deficient, a person could feel a lack of will power, resolve and contentment.

Health In excess, metal chi can lead to constriction of the lungs and increase the risk of constipation. It will also contribute to feeling tight, stiff and tense, and can result in headaches.

When metal chi is deficient, there can be a risk of problems in assimilating food and oxygen.

Water

This is the element of night-time and winter energy – flowing, flexible and spreading. This is the energy of stars, dark and cold. Imagine standing in a field at midnight looking up at the stars, seeing the vastness of the universe while

A bony face with small eyes, thin lips and a pinched nose contribute to a metal chi appearance.

also being aware of the silence around you and your own body. Here, looking up at the night sky, you become aware of the size of the universe and can look at your own problems in a new perspective.

Character Water energy in a person is helpful for feeling objective, flexible and peaceful. It can help you feel independent and is a great chi for regeneration and healing. This chi is useful for accessing your deepest feelings.

In excess, it can lead to being secretive, evasive and fearful. It is an energy that helps mix with people from all kinds of backgrounds and enjoy a wide variety of situations. Water chi can help a person see the big picture while exploring subjects deeply.

Mysterious deep-set eyes, a deep philtrum and thin expressive eyebrows are signs of the strength of water chi.

When water chi is deficient, a person risks losing power and vitality. In this situation someone might seem empty and lifeless.

Health In excess, water chi increases the risk of producing too much adrenalin, swellings, feeling cold, night sweats and clammy skin.

When deficient, water chi can lead to a lack of sexual vitality, loss of strength and poor recovery from illness.

A deficiency of water chi is also considered to increase the risk of bladder and kidney infections.

Constitution

When face reading, it is important to distinguish whether the feature of a face that you are looking at reflects someone's constitution. These are aspects of the face that will change very little during adulthood.

This woman's oval face shape, large eyes and cleft chin are constitutional features that will not change naturally over time.

An example of an unchanging feature would be the bones of the skull. Once formed there is unlikely to be any drastic change. These bones will define the basic shape of the face and influence our face reading. As the bones are unlikely to change, we need to recognize that the information we derive about someone due to the face shape is also unlikely to change.

These features of the face reflect aspects of our character that are innate and part of our DNA. For example, an oval-shaped face might indicate that a person is creative and this would be something that would remain a part of that person's character.

Similarly, these constitutional facial features will reflect potential strengths or weaknesses in terms of health that will always be there. For example, if someone is born with a weak heart then this is likely to always be an issue. It may be possible to overcome the problem by eating a healthy diet and regular stretching but there will always be the risk that the problem will reoccur if precautions are not maintained.

Reading behind cosmetic surgery

One problem with which traditional face readers did not have to contend was cosmetic surgery. This can be misleading and may distort a reading. If you notice evidence of cosmetic surgery, try to estimate how the face would have looked before its alteration. In terms of character there is the dilemma as to whether the person had the cosmetic surgery in order that his or her face better reflected the character inside or simply in order to look younger or feel closer to current trends in beauty.

WHAT TO LOOK FOR

Face shape Once a person has reached his or her late teens the bones of the skull will not change much and the face shape becomes set.

Forehead In terms of shape the forehead will not change in adulthood.

Eyes The size, colour of the pupils and spacing of the eyes will not change and are constitutional features.

Nose The nose can continue to grow slowly and the tip might become more bulbous with age; however, this process is too slow to reflect any change in someone's condition and I would therefore consider this to be part of a person's constitution.

Ears The ears continue to grow slowly; however, their general shape and position on the side of the head will not change enough to reflect someone's day-to-day condition.

Lips The lips tend to get thinner with age. Again this is a slow process and the size and shape of the lips can be considered to reflect a person's constitution.

Jaw The jaw will not change significantly in adulthood and it will therefore reflect someone's constitution.

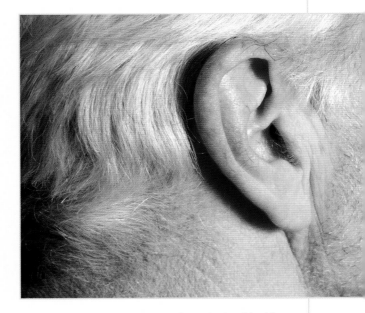

The ears can be a good indicator of constitutional health. They will naturally be larger in an older person.

Note When looking at the nose, ears and lips in terms of someone's constitution it is important to take into account his or her age as these features will change slowly with age.

Condition

A person's condition is reflected in things that change. For example, you might notice your complexion changes from one day to the next or that a pimple emerges temporarily. These will pass and simply reflect your state at the time.

One of the challenges of face reading is being able to discern what might be a temporary one-off mark or something that is a regular occurrence. This will be easy to see in your own face and in the face of someone who you see regularly but harder in a person you are seeing for the first time.

Someone may have experienced changes in his or her face due to scarring, burns or broken bones. These may leave a permanent mark on the face. There is a theory that the subject might have attracted these events and therefore the visual residue as a result of some imbalance in his or her own physical or emotional health at the time. I do not subscribe to this theory wholeheartedly, but it is interesting to note where these marks are and to what they related. I might use this to prompt questions and see if there is any connection between his or her condition at the time and the way the injuries affected the face.

Face-altering changes

We often cha[...] Applying make-up woul[...] could also take the form [...]ying false eyelashes, sh[...]ng. It is interesting to [...]s to do this as part of a f[...]ill certainly tell us more a[...]

Make-up can make face reading harder but it can provide clues in itself. Here the subject has added a fiery colour to her lips, perhaps wanting to be more expressive.

WHAT TO LOOK FOR

Hair It is possible to make some form of character analysis based on hairstyles. In addition the hair will often influence the look of a person's face. Hair will change in terms of colour and quantity with age.

Lines and wrinkles These come under the category of the face we deserve as sometimes lines will form according to the kind of facial expressions we make. Laughter lines running up from the sides of the mouth would be a good example. In addition, lines and wrinkles are affected by the climate in which the individual lives. Hot, dry, sunny climates increase the incidence of wrinkles.

Eyebrows Plucking eyebrows is the most common change and this will tell us more about a person's character and how he or she wants to be perceived. Eyebrows will become more bushy with age and change colour.

Eyes The whites of the eyes will change and may become bloodshot or yellow depending on the person's current state of health.

Complexion Skin colour can change quickly from red to blotchy to looking sallow. This can provide interesting information on the individual's current emotional state and health.

Cheeks A blush can come and go in seconds providing useful clues as to a person's feelings and, if this is a regular occurrence, health. Over time a person can become gaunt, looking thin in the cheeks or at another stage in life may appear puffed up across the cheeks reflecting different states of health.

Tip of nose The tip of the nose can change colour, typically becoming redder, pale or even slightly purple.

In this face the most obvious signs of condition are the darker colour, lines and swelling below the eyes.

Lips The lips can change colour quickly reflecting changes in a person's emotional state and his or her current health condition.

Ears The ears can redden and experience a burning sensation reflecting a current health condition.

Spots and pimples These will come and go but in some people there may be a long history of pimples developing in a particular part of the face providing more clues to current health.

Chapter 2

FACES

Over the next few pages, you will find descriptions of each type of face and and an analysis of the features of the face in order to determine which of the five elements is more prevalent in a person. This chapter will reveal all you need to know in order to make a basic face reading. You might find it helpful to refer back to this chapter to refresh yourself with the simple overall basics of making a five-element face reading.

The wood face

By examining the shape of the face, then scrutinizing the features, complexion and expression in turn, you will gain an insight into what constitutes the wood face.

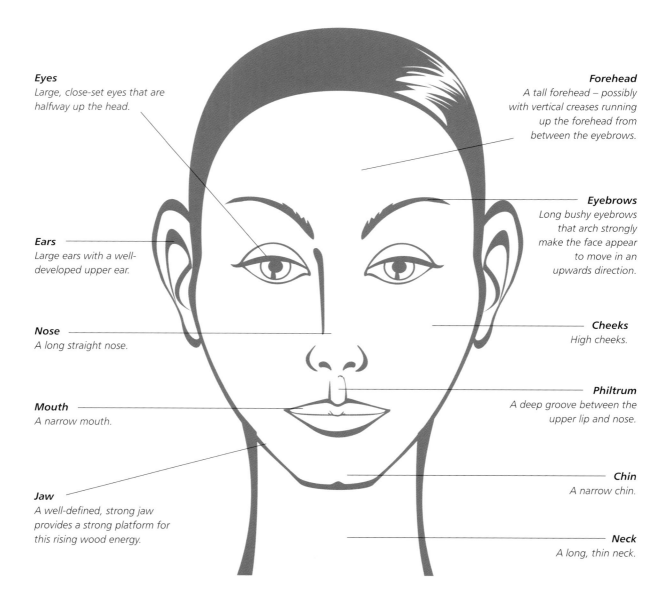

Eyes
Large, close-set eyes that are halfway up the head.

Forehead
A tall forehead – possibly with vertical creases running up the forehead from between the eyebrows.

Eyebrows
Long bushy eyebrows that arch strongly make the face appear to move in an upwards direction.

Ears
Large ears with a well-developed upper ear.

Cheeks
High cheeks.

Nose
A long straight nose.

Philtrum
A deep groove between the upper lip and nose.

Mouth
A narrow mouth.

Chin
A narrow chin.

Jaw
A well-defined, strong jaw provides a strong platform for this rising wood energy.

Neck
A long, thin neck.

Shape

A wood-shaped face is characterized by a tall forehead and the eyes might appear to be halfway up the head. Often the whole head will appear tall and narrow, and this can be emphasized by a narrow but strong jaw. A receding hairline accentuates the forehead so you will need to imagine the person with no hair to be consistent. If you are looking at a friend consider masking off the hair with your hands.

If you stand back and relax your gaze, a person with plenty of wood chi will appear to have energy moving vertically up his or her face.

Features

The eyebrows and jaw are considered prime features in terms of seeing wood energy. Long bushy eyebrows and a strong jaw line will indicate a greater presence of wood chi. Looking at the mouth, nose and eyes you will notice these features combine to form a vertical emphasis running up the centre of the face.

Complexion

Wood chi creates an olive, slightly yellow, complexion. Such a person will tend not to flush easily.

Expression

This person will come across as focused and able to concentrate. A typical person with a lot of wood energy will hold your stare and feel comfortable talking directly into your face. Such a person will look up often and you may notice that you can see the whites of his or her eye below the pupil. He or she

will be expressive in the forehead. You may notice a raising of the eyebrows, frowning and movement along the hairline.

Characteristics

This sunrise, spring time energy flows up through the body to the head forming pools of activity in the brain. This can help someone be mentally active with great powers of reasoning and logic. Because of the vertical narrow flow this mental energy tends to be focused and can be concentrated on details. As this energy rises quickly such a person can find his or her enthusiasm takes off quickly and may find feelings of impatience or irritation surface suddenly. Wood chi is associated with anger in Chinese five-element medicine. However, people with plenty of wood energy tend to be positive and up, responding to challenges easily.

A tall forehead, upward-arched eyebrows and vertical creases between the eyebrows give Jamie Lee Curtis the appearance of having strong wood chi.

The fire face

Round, full cheeks, large, radiant eyes and a readiness to blush characterize the fire face. Openness and expressiveness are represented on this face and are a reflection of this individual's temperament.

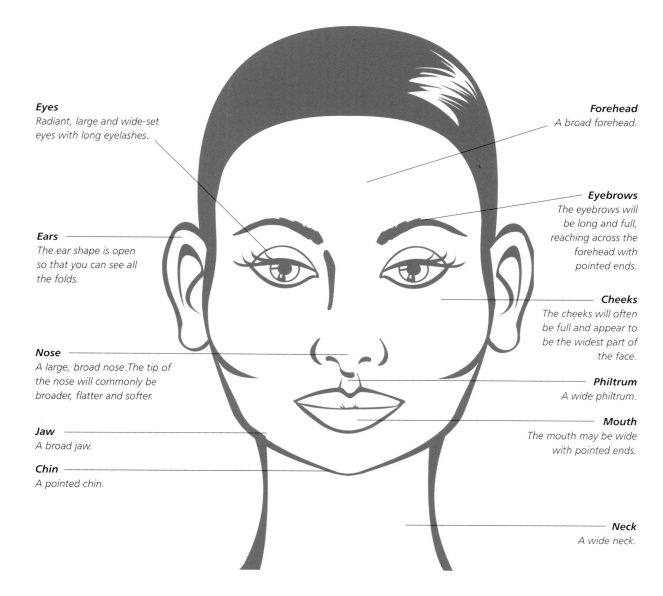

Eyes
Radiant, large and wide-set eyes with long eyelashes.

Forehead
A broad forehead.

Eyebrows
The eyebrows will be long and full, reaching across the forehead with pointed ends.

Ears
The ear shape is open so that you can see all the folds.

Cheeks
The cheeks will often be full and appear to be the widest part of the face.

Nose
A large, broad nose. The tip of the nose will commonly be broader, flatter and softer.

Philtrum
A wide philtrum.

Mouth
The mouth may be wide with pointed ends.

Jaw
A broad jaw.

Chin
A pointed chin.

Neck
A wide neck.

Shape

A fire-shaped face will be round with full cheeks. The widest part of the face will be at the level of the bridge of the nose. When you first look at a person with a fire-shaped face the cheeks will stand out.

This face can be masked by long hair falling across the sides of the face and you may need to ask the person to pull back his or her hair to be sure. A strong fringe can make a face appear rounder so lift the hair off the forehead to make an accurate assessment.

A face radiating fire chi will appear to have energy spreading out to the periphery making the surface of the face more reactive and expressive.

Features

The main fire features are the eyes and tip of the nose. Features with an abundance of fire chi will be spread out and are larger. Strong laughter lines along with creases around the outsides of the eyes are typical.

Complexion

Fire chi is hot and radiant and will show up as a reddish face prone to flush easily. Usually a person with strong fire energy will find his or her complexion will change quickly, expressing internal emotions.

Expression

A typical person with a lot of fire energy will be open, fiery, engaging, animated and dynamic.

You will see a lot of movement in the face, whether in the eyes, mouth or cheeks. Eyes will tend to flit around quickly and open widely when excited. Such a person will make eye contact but then play by

making and breaking contact. These people smile readily and react quickly to changes in mood.

Characteristics

A face with these fire features suggests that the person enjoys a history of radiating fire chi. This midday, summer energy flows out from the heart and mind actively. This spreads emotions out to the surface quickly and makes such a person easy to read in terms of emotions.

Fire energy reacts quickly, spreading out, energizing the skin and then retracting quickly when the mood changes. This can make a fire chi person interesting to observe. Fire chi is associated with hysteria in Chinese five-element medicine. However, people with plenty of fire chi often have excellent people skills and are able to bond deeply with others on an emotional level.

Sarah Ferguson's broad forehead, full cheeks and radiant smile create a strong fire-energy appearance.

The earth face

This face type is typified by a wide jaw and generous mouth, a reflection of the tendency for earth chi people to be steady and down-to-earth.

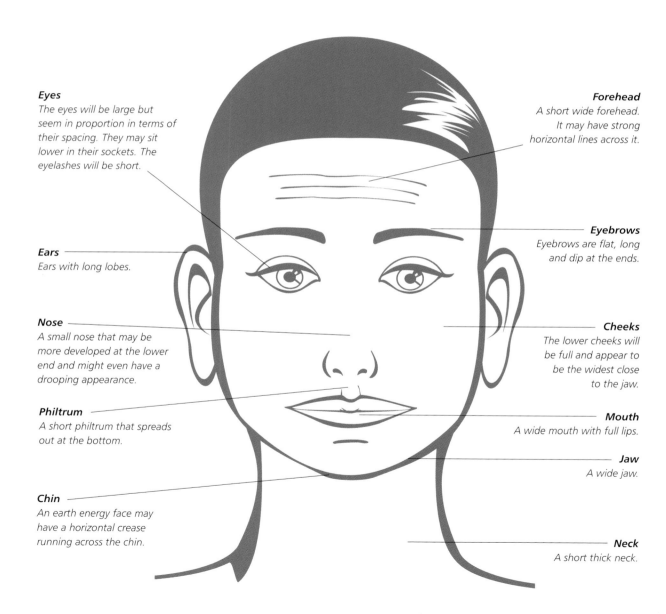

Eyes
The eyes will be large but seem in proportion in terms of their spacing. They may sit lower in their sockets. The eyelashes will be short.

Ears
Ears with long lobes.

Nose
A small nose that may be more developed at the lower end and might even have a drooping appearance.

Philtrum
A short philtrum that spreads out at the bottom.

Chin
An earth energy face may have a horizontal crease running across the chin.

Forehead
A short wide forehead. It may have strong horizontal lines across it.

Eyebrows
Eyebrows are flat, long and dip at the ends.

Cheeks
The lower cheeks will be full and appear to be the widest close to the jaw.

Mouth
A wide mouth with full lips.

Jaw
A wide jaw.

Neck
A short thick neck.

Shape

An earth-shaped face will reflect settling energy. The strongest part of the face is the mouth and lower cheeks and it is typically emphasized by a wide jaw. Ears with long lobes and/or ears that are set lower on the face will confirm a strong flow of earth chi. A well-formed chin will add to the feeling that the energy flows downwards. A beard can accentuate an earth-shape, so you'll need to imagine the person clean-shaven for consistency.

Features

The mouth is the prime earth chi feature drawing a strong horizontal line across the lower part of the face. Full wide lips indicate a strong presence of earth energy. A face with an abundance of earth chi will have an appearance of solidity and security.

Complexion

Earth chi is relatively slow and steady with the result that a person with plenty of this energy will tend to change colour less easily. In a healthy person the skin tones would classically be made up of pinks.

Expression

A person who has an abundance of earth energy will come across as steady, secure and stable. A typical person with a lot of earth energy will be methodical, practical and down-to-earth. You will see movement in the face concentrated around the mouth and jaw. He or she will tend to look down and choose words carefully. Such a person will make eye contact but often for shorter periods. People with a predominance of earth chi can appear shy and take longer to open up.

Kate Winslet's full lips, wide forehead with faint horizontal lines and wide jaw are earth energy features.

Characteristics

A face with these earth features suggests the person has led a life that is predicated around being practical and doing the right thing. This afternoon, late-summer energy flows down from the mind through the stomach and middle organs. This creates a strong connection between the body and mind, making it more satisfying to use the mind in ways that result in something tangible and real.

As earth energy filters down, a person experiencing this energy may appear a little slow and cautious at times. Quality is more important than quantity. This can make an earth person harder to get to know and less noticeable in a crowd. Earth chi is associated with jealous. However, people with plenty of earth chi are often highly reliable, perceptive, considerate and thoughtful.

The metal face

A metal-shaped face will reflect inward-flowing energy. This will show up as a face that looks contained, dignified and somewhat expressionless.

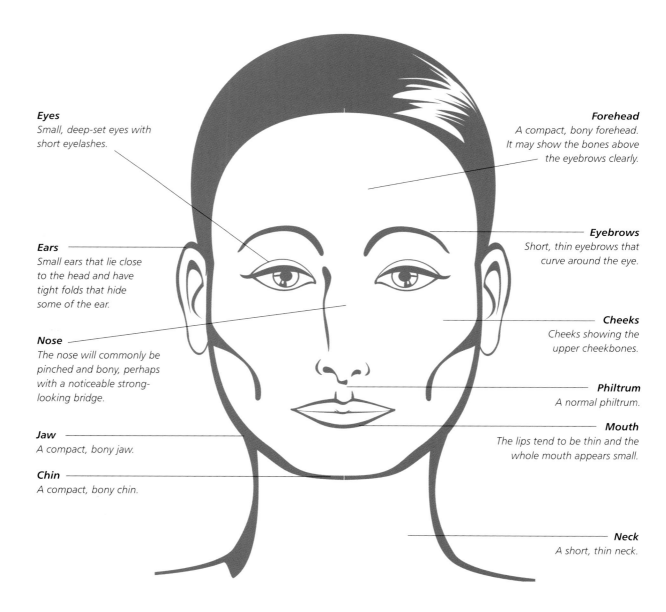

Eyes
Small, deep-set eyes with short eyelashes.

Ears
Small ears that lie close to the head and have tight folds that hide some of the ear.

Nose
The nose will commonly be pinched and bony, perhaps with a noticeable strong-looking bridge.

Jaw
A compact, bony jaw.

Chin
A compact, bony chin.

Forehead
A compact, bony forehead. It may show the bones above the eyebrows clearly.

Eyebrows
Short, thin eyebrows that curve around the eye.

Cheeks
Cheeks showing the upper cheekbones.

Philtrum
A normal philtrum.

Mouth
The lips tend to be thin and the whole mouth appears small.

Neck
A short, thin neck.

Shape

This face with its inward-flowing energy is typically emphasized by deep eyes, flat or sunken cheeks and more bony features. Ears that lie close to the head with a tight formation will confirm the subject has a strong flow of metal chi. A metal-shaped face can be accentuated by shaving the head. If you know someone well try placing a wig over his or her head to see the difference.

A person with a metal chi face will retain energy, giving the appearance of someone with an inner steel and deep resources.

Features

Key metal features are the nose and cheekbones. This central region across the face will reveal how well someone holds and contains energy. The features will contribute to the appearance of a self-assured face. The cheeks will often be sunken emphasizing the cheekbones. In extremes there may be vertical creases running up the cheeks.

Complexion

Metal chi draws itself inwards with the result that such a person can look pale and in extremes slightly grey.

Expression

A person with an abundance of metal energy will be slightly withdrawn, contained and less likely to give facial clues to his or her feelings. This person will often be a good listener, reserved, elegant and noble.

People with an excess of metal chi do not give much back in terms of expression and can seem aloof.

Gwyneth Paltrow has high cheekbones, a more bony face and compact features. This suggests a greater presence of metal chi.

Some people will find them slightly intimidating as the metal person just seems to be taking it all in without making a response.

Characteristics

A face with these metal features suggests the person has led a life that is predicated around developing the inner self. This evening, autumn energy flows in from the periphery. This creates a deep sensitivity to other people and the surrounding environment.

As metal energy filters inwards a person experiencing this energy will tend to appear more withdrawn at times. This can make them seem distant and slightly untouchable. Metal chi is associated with grief in Chinese five-element medicine. However, people with plenty of metal chi are often highly resourceful, intuitive, attractive and interesting.

The water face

Delicate features, twinkly eyes and translucent skin are indications of a water face; this type is the most difficult to read.

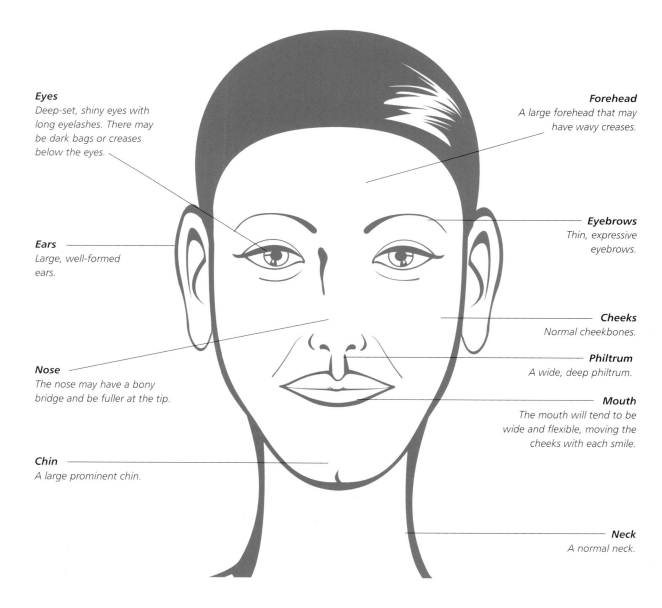

Eyes
Deep-set, shiny eyes with long eyelashes. There may be dark bags or creases below the eyes.

Ears
Large, well-formed ears.

Nose
The nose may have a bony bridge and be fuller at the tip.

Chin
A large prominent chin.

Forehead
A large forehead that may have wavy creases.

Eyebrows
Thin, expressive eyebrows.

Cheeks
Normal cheekbones.

Philtrum
A wide, deep philtrum.

Mouth
The mouth will tend to be wide and flexible, moving the cheeks with each smile.

Neck
A normal neck.

Shape

A water-shaped face will reflect energy flowing more randomly and looks flexible and changeable with chameleon-like qualities. Typically, this quality is emphasized by a mouth that appear sensual and moves easily, eyes that twinkle and translucent skin. A face formed with strong water chi will appear slightly delicate with fine features.

This face type can be the hardest to read as the person may have a wide range of facial expressions. Watch over a period of time to see the changes.

Features

The main features that reflect water chi are the ears and chin. An abundance of water chi will contribute to the appearance of a deep, sensitive face. The ears will appear refined with well-defined curving lines.

Complexion

Water chi flows easily with the result that a person with plenty of this energy can have a pale translucent-looking skin. In extremes it may take on a purple hue close to the corners of the eyes.

Expression

A water chi person will come across as easy-going and adaptable. This man or woman will find it easy to interact with a wide range of people from very different backgrounds. Typically such a person will be engaging, deep and affectionate.

People with plenty of water chi smile easily and you will notice their faces appear to move a lot. Sometimes this can make them seem slightly nervous.

Renée Zellweger's well-defined ears, slightly transluscent skin and strong prominent chin are signs of powerful water chi.

You may find your gaze is held by the person using his or her mouth and eyes.

Characteristics

A face with water features suggests that the person has led a life where he or she has found flexibility to be a successful strategy. A water person can easily adapt to his or her surroundings. This night, winter energy combines the deepest core energy with more superficial chi. The result is an interesting mix of deep thoughts and emotions with being accessible and open.

As water energy flows easily a person experiencing this energy will tend to enjoy a wide range of interests and like variety. Often this leads to an interest in spiritual activities. Water chi is associated with fear in Chinese five-element medicine. However, these people are often original, fascinating, good company.

Chapter 3

THE KEY FIVE-ELEMENT FEATURES

Hone your face-reading skills by examining more closely how the key features of the face can reveal additional clues about someone's character. These are useful features to practise on initially. Remember to try and make a point of comparing a hundred different noses and then move on to mouths, eyes, cheeks, eyebrows and ears so that you become familiar with each feature and confident with your observational skills.

Cheeks

The colour, texture, shape and the presence of spots, lines or blemishes can all affect the interpretation of the cheeks in face reading.

Oriental medicine

In terms of traditional Oriental medicine the cheeks relate to the lungs. The cheeks reveal information on how effective the lungs are at transferring oxygen into the blood and expelling carbon dioxide. This literally tells us how a person interacts with the air but in a broader sense reveals how someone interacts emotionally with people around them. The upper cheeks tell us more about the presence of metal chi and the lower cheeks provide information on earth energy.

Emotion

The cheeks tell us how someone expresses him or herself emotionally and provides clues as to how someone is feeling emotionally. The cheeks respond quickly to elevated emotions by turning red or becoming pale.

How to observe

Observe the cheeks from different angles, ideally in daylight. The cheeks should be free from foundation, rouge or any recent application of moisturizer. Watch how the cheeks change with a smile. Be aware that cold weather may cause the cheeks to redden.

Making a reading

Look at the cheeks and work through looking at the bone structure, then the coloration and finally the condition of the skin. Check the cheeks for any lines and creases.

See if the form of the cheeks matches the coloration. For example, full cheeks with a reddish complexion will confirm a fire chi condition or sunken cheeks with a grey complexion strongly suggests the presence of metal chi.

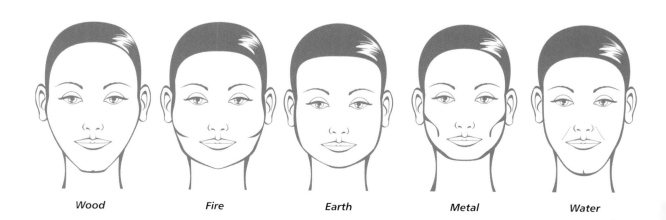

Wood   *Fire*   *Earth*   *Metal*   *Water*

WHAT TO LOOK FOR

Full cheeks If the cheeks look full it indicates the subject is able to express his or her emotions easily and connect emotionally with other people. This helps create strong emotional bonds with friends and makes such a person appear warm and friendly. This is typical of a person with more fire chi.

Sunken cheeks If the cheeks appear sunken or the cheekbones are obvious the person may find it harder to express emotional feelings. This suggests that the person is more likely to hold on to feelings and feel withdrawn when experiencing difficult emotions. This is a feature that is typical of someone with more metal chi.

Vertical lines This is a rare mark but indicates a strong desire to hold on to certain emotions and feelings for better or worse. It reflects a strong presence of metal chi.

Red complexion Red cheeks in normal temperatures reflect increased activity in the energy of interaction. This might be due to a desire to express emotions or feeling frustrated about the ability to share emotions or not being understood emotionally. Such a condition suggests an abundance of fire chi.

Sallow appearance A pale skin colour indicates less desire to express emotions and interact. Such a person could feel content and happy within him or herself. This would be more typical when there is a greater presence of earth chi or if there is a slight translucent quality, more water chi. An orange hue can suggest a more stuck condition where there might be a feeling of wanting to express emotions such as anger but suppressing these urges. This should not be confused with a more olive complexion on the cheeks that would allow a free expression of anger and reflect more wood chi.

Grey colour Pale or whitish-coloured cheeks with a hint of grey indicate more severe feelings of isolation, loneliness and perhaps depression. This would be more acute if accompanied by sunken cheeks. Such a condition suggests a stronger presence of metal chi.

Blush Blushing is commonly associated with feelings of embarrassment but could also be associated with excitement or sexual arousal. It represents fire chi. This is a quick temporary response to emotional stimulation and indicates emotions come up to the surface easily.

Spots If the cheeks are a regular location for spots or pimples this sometimes indicates that the person has a slight discomfort in expressing emotions and is an indication of metal chi.

Here the subject's cheeks appear full and rosy suggesting a presence of fire chi and an ease at expressing emotions.

Eyebrows

The shape, length, thickness and position of the eyebrows is important in facing reading, as is the way in which the person may move the eyebrows to make a point.

Oriental medicine

In terms of traditional Oriental medicine, the eyebrows relate to three different stages of life. The inner third to youth, the middle third to middle age and the outer third to old age. This gives clues to the way in which someone's life will develop. The eyebrows provide insights into the way wood chi moves in the body.

Emotion

The eyebrows reflect someone's depth of character and personality. They also provide helpful clues as to how the subject treats other people.

How to observe

Eyebrows are easier to observe as they stand out. Look at the shape, length, thickness and position of the eyebrows. Also spend enough time with someone to see how he or she uses the eyebrows. Plucked eyebrows create a metal appearance. Shorter, thinner eyebrows create the look of being more confined with energy moving inwards. Consider where the eyebrows look strongest and think about which part of his or her life it corresponds to.

Making a reading

Watch the eyebrows while they are still and observe the length, thickness, position and shape. Then observe the eyebrows when the person is expressing him or herself. Strong upward movements would suggest more wood energy, expressive movements more fire chi, downward movements more earth energy, frowning more metal chi and easy flowing movements more water energy.

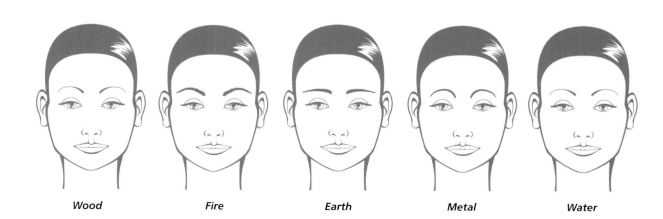

Wood   *Fire*   *Earth*   *Metal*   *Water*

WHAT TO LOOK FOR

Length The length of eyebrow gives clues to a person's perseverance and tenacity. The longer the eyebrows the better the individual is able to stick with a challenge. Shorter eyebrows suggest that the person will get impatient and have a greater desire to move on to something else if the current situation is not working out.

Thickness Thick, bushy eyebrows reflect a strong personality, especially when combined with long eyebrows. Such a person can make a memorable impression through his or her strength of character. This may be through a quiet, deep energy that gives the impression of power without expressing it or making any effort to project this strength. Thinner eyebrows indicate a person is more flexible and better at adapting and finding new ways to overcome a problem. Such a person can be more reactive in social situations, especially if the eyebrows also arch noticeably.

Position A wide gap between the eyebrows suggests someone who likes variety and change but might be easily distracted. In extreme cases, this indicates a somewhat dualistic character where the person can exhibit a wide range of character traits. A small gap between the eyebrows is associated with single-mindedness.

Shape Although eyebrows generally relate to wood chi we can see the other five-element energies within the eyebrows:

• **Wood-shaped** eyebrows arch up strongly and often the outer end will be higher than the inner end. This indicates that the person is assertive, dynamic and ambitious. Such a person might find slower people frustrating to the point of irritation.

These eyebrows exhibit a water chi quality, being thin, long and uneven.

• **Fire-shaped** eyebrows are long, bushy and with a wider space between. They are expressive and catch your attention. Such a person will find it easy to project emotions and others will sense his or her mood.

• **Earth-shaped** eyebrows will be flat across the face and drop down at the outer ends. These eyebrows suggest a considerate, patient and thoughtful person. It is likely that such a person will be sympathetic.

• **Metal-shaped** eyebrows arch up and curve around the eye. They may also be shorter, hugging the contours of the bone around the eye. This indicates the person will be self-contained, a good listener and receptive to ideas.

• **Water-shaped** eyebrows are thin and spread across the face. These may be broken and can be faint and harder to see. Such a person will find it easy to adapt to the people around him or her and be flexible in terms of conversation.

Eyes

When it comes to analyzing the eyes, shape, size, placing within the socket and even blink rate give clues to the person behind these windows to the soul.

Oriental medicine

In terms of traditional Oriental medicine, the eyes relate to the nervous system. In addition the whites of the eyes can give clues to the condition of the liver. As a whole the eyes tell us more about the presence and flow of fire chi through a person.

Emotion

The eyes are said to be the window to the soul and through the eyes we can see deep into someone's emotional energy. It is by looking into someone's eyes that we feel that we really connect.

How to observe

The pupils can change quickly as can the aperture of the eyelids, the blink rate and eye movement, making the eyes extremely interesting to observe. However, because the eyes are so changeable they need to be monitored for some time to gain enough information to make an accurate reading.

As an interesting exercise, cut out a wide rectangle in a piece of card so that when held in front of the face so you can only see the eyes. Ask a friend to hold the card up and continue with a conversation. You will now be highly aware of the person's eye movements.

You might find that some people actually look frightened with this exercise as their eyes flit around the room.

Making a reading

Look at the eyes straight on and from a similar height to make an accurate and consistent reading. Work through the list opposite and base your reading on any aspects that make the biggest impression on you.

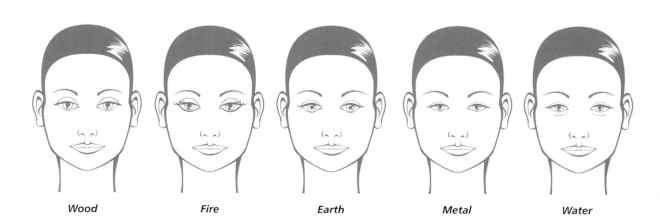

Wood　　　　*Fire*　　　　*Earth*　　　　*Metal*　　　　*Water*

WHAT TO LOOK FOR

Spacing Eyes that are spaced further apart are associated with a greater presence of expansive fire chi. In terms of the eyes it can mean someone tends to enjoy variety, be open-minded, like to see the big picture and have a large vision of life. At the same time, such a person may become easily distracted, unfocused and lose direction. Eyes that are closer together would suggest more inward metal chi. When related to the position of the eyes it suggests the person will be focused, direct and accurate with enhanced powers of concentration. This person may also miss opportunities by being too narrow-minded.

Size Larger eyes indicate a greater presence of wood or fire chi. In respect of the eyes this indicates a more open, accessible personality that is easier to get to know. We associate large eyes with someone who is kind and gentle. Smaller eyes would suggest more earth and metal chi. When applied to the eyes this relates to being

perceptive, direct and deep. Such a person can be intimidating if the surrounding features feel compacted around the eyes, especially if accompanied by a vertical crease between the eyebrows.

Bulging or sunken eyes Bulging eyes, indicating more fire chi, suggest the person is broad-minded and interested in new experiences but may appear intense in terms of interacting with others. Sunken eyes, pointing to more metal and or water chi, are associated with a tendency to be more withdrawn and secretive.

Position within sockets When the pupil appears higher up in the socket so you see the white of the eye below the pupil there is a greater presence of wood chi. This up chi suggests a tendency to get lost in dreams and space out. If the pupil is lower in the socket so you see the white of the eye above the pupil there is increased flow of earth chi indicating a strength in terms of being down-to-earth and practical.

Watering eyes Eyes that appear shiny, watery or moist indicate a greater presence of water chi. You might best see this where the eye meets the lower eyelid. This is often associated with vitality and zest for life but in extreme cases suggests anxiety.

Movement Be aware of changes in eye movement. Someone whose eyes move a lot indicates a tendency to be distracted and easily bored. This can be due to anxiety, nervousness or feeling ill-at-ease. Slower eye movements or holding your gaze suggests a more relaxed, calm state and the ability to focus.

This person's right eye is slightly larger, suggesting greater openess in creativity, art and imagination.

Nose

Once again, we are looking at the size, shape and position of the nose in relation to the other features on the face, in order to competently read the face.

Oriental medicine

In traditional Oriental medicine, the tip of the nose relates to the heart. The heart moves blood around the body and is also thought to be where we most feel our emotions. The heart chi spreads emotional energy. In terms of the five elements the tip of the nose reflects fire chi while the middle bridge tells us more about the activity of metal chi in a person. This provides clues as to the state of the lungs.

Emotion

The tip of the nose tells us how someone deals with emotional feelings and provides clues as to how he or she will express them. The bridge presents clues as to how someone holds on to his or her emotions and the strength of that person's resolve.

How to observe

Look at the nose from the front and in profile. Examine the size, shape and position of the nose relative to the mouth and eyes. Pay attention to the tip of the nose to see if there is a cleft or any change in coloration. Make a mental note of the subject's general complexion.

Making a reading

Look at the subject's nose face on and in profile. Work through the list of things to observe opposite and make a careful note of the constitutional indications – this would be the cartilage. Then move on to thinking about the way the nose reflects the person's current condition – here you can look at the colour and skin quality.

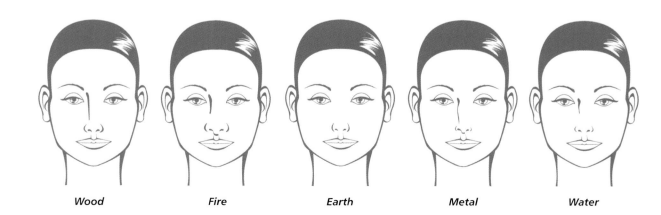

Wood   *Fire*   *Earth*   *Metal*   *Water*

WHAT TO LOOK FOR

Shape in profile A high bridge or even an outward curve suggest that the person has drive and ambition. Often this will be focused on creating greater material wealth. Such a person may be good at attracting people into his or her fold. A smaller nose with a low bridge indicates the subject will be a good team worker and is happy to achieve as part of a group. A larger, rounded tip suggests the person experiences strong emotions and may be emotionally led, making decisions on how he or she feels at the time.

Shape face on A narrow bridge indicates the person will hold on to thoughts and emotions and find it harder to forgive or let go. At the same time he or she will have a clear direction in life. A broad nose at the bridge shows a quiet strength and this could be someone who can come to the fore in a crisis. A pinched or narrow tip suggests the person tends to focus his or her emotions tightly on a few people or issues in life. A wide tip indicates someone will not only have strong emotions but that they will spread them widely to include many different people and issues. Such a person can appear to be free-flowing emotionally.
• **A wood-shaped** nose will appear shorter and higher on the face with a bigger gap between the mouth and nose. In profile the nose may appear to turn up.
• **A fire-shaped** nose will appear to spread out when looking from the front and tend to be larger at the tip.
• **An earth-shaped** nose may droop slightly and be set low on the face with a small gap between nose and mouth.
• **A metal-shaped** nose will have a strong bony bridge but appear smaller and look pinched at the tip.
• **A water-shaped** nose will be soft and appear to be fleshy. In profile it may have a slight wave along the bridge.

A strong rounded middle bridge of the nose indicates that this woman has drive and ambition to succeed.

Cleft A cleft suggests a slightly discordant personality that can quickly change and display different traits.

Coloration A nose that gets purple at its tip would indicate that the subject finds it difficult to control his or her emotions with the risk of fiery outbursts. A reddish nose indicates the person feels comfortable expressing him or herself emotionally, whereas a pale nose suggests that the person needs to find someone trustworthy before opening up. Such a person would tend to be more withdrawn emotionally.

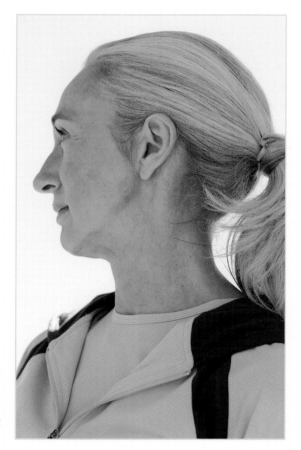

Mouth

On one level, the mouth is simply the way to the stomach, while on another, it determines the attitude to responsibility and fun.

Oriental medicine

In traditional Oriental medicine, the mouth relates to the digestive system. It is the opening to your stomach. In terms of the five elements the mouth reflects earth chi and is associated with the stomach, spleen and pancreas.

Emotion

The mouth tells us about someone's sensuality. It is where we kiss and kissing can be a prelude to sex and greater intimacy.

The mouth also displays secrets relating to approach to work. The mouth is associated with hunger and the urge to go out to work. Here you can read more about someone's attitude to responsibility, commitments and having fun.

How to observe

You need time to observe the mouth as it is highly mobile and will look very different depending on whether the person is smiling, serious or talking. The shape of the lips will change radically if they are pursed, puckered or pouting. Watch someone for long enough to see a full range of lip shapes.

Making a reading

Practise reading the mouth when it is completely relaxed and then go on to reading smiles and the mouth in motion. Try different topics of conversation to see if certain emotions result in different movements in the mouth. You might notice that the lips become pale if the person is nervous or that they become thinner if the person is anxious.

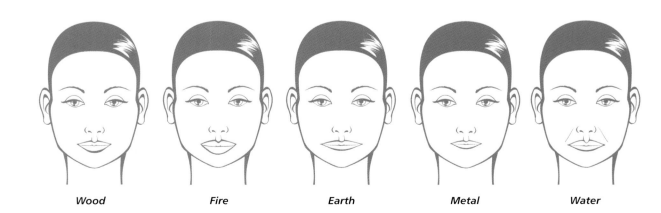

Wood　　　*Fire*　　　*Earth*　　　*Metal*　　　*Water*

WHAT TO LOOK FOR

Wide mouth A wide mouth indicates a strong appetite for life and a hunger for new experiences. Such a person will find it harder to feel satisfied and once settled get the urge to institute changes. Earth and fire elements are present.

Narrow mouth More contained energy and a person who is better able to make the most of whatever he or she has is suggested here. This person will have a greater appreciation for modesty, austerity and simplicity. Metal element is present.

Full lips Lips that are full indicate someone who enjoys the pleasures of life and is likely to be funloving and will make the most of life as it happens. These lips suggest the person values sensual experiences. Fire element is present.

Thin lips Thin lips are associated with being more serious, responsible and hard working. Such a person may judge him or herself harshly and similarly expect high standards from others. Metal element is present.

Curvy lips Lips that have a strong curvy shape across the top of the upper lip and a noticeable curve along the lower edge of the bottom lip indicate that style and artistic qualities are important. Water element is present.

Open mouth Someone who leaves his or her mouth open may have an excess of earth chi. This can indicate a heaviness in thought with greater emphasis on the practical side of life.

This person's lower lip is pale, suggesting a lack of inner energy. In contrast, there is some flushing on the middle upper lip, which indicates a possible overactivity of the stomach.

Red lips A strong red colour in the lips indicates a more fiery condition or fire element, where the person may be excited, aroused or feel stimulated.

Pale lips Pale lips suggest someone who may be feeling withdrawn and disinterested in sensory experiences and have an excess of metal chi. Such a person may be feeling vulnerable and insecure.

Purple lips You may sometimes see a purple patch on the lower part of the upper lip. This would suggest the person is not particularly satisfied on a sensory level. There may be an excess of earth or fire chi.

Mouth in motion Someone who opens his or her mouth widely when talking will have a greater desire to interact and feel more at ease revealing aspects about his or her character. Using the lips obviously when talking to help make the right sounds displays a desire to be understood verbally and emotionally as well as a tendency to want to dictate thoughts to others.

Conversely, anyone who mumbles or talks with his or her mouth partially closed will be less open or expressive. He or she may prefer to keep some distance before getting to know a person.

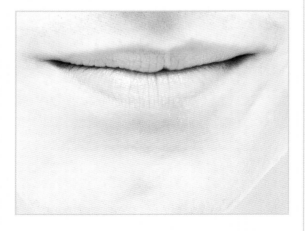

Ears

These features tell us about spirit, courage and how a person meets the challenges of life, his or her vitality and ability to heal.

Oriental medicine

In traditional Oriental medicine, the ears relate to the kidneys, bladder and adrenal glands. In terms of the five elements the ears reflect water chi, which is concerned with vitality, sex and conception.

In addition, water chi is vital for healing and regeneration. Large ears are traditionally considered a sign of longevity and a strong constitution.

As ears continue to grow large ears have been used as a sign of age and wisdom in societies where birth dates were not recorded.

Emotion

The ears tell us more about someone's zest for life, courage and ability to take on challenges.

How to observe

Look at the ears face on and in profile. Look carefully at the shape of the ears, their position on the head, whether they are flat or stick out. Pay particular attention to whether the ears look more developed at the top part or at the lobes.

Making a reading

Work through the list opposite to make your reading. Make sure long hair is pulled well back and see the ears in context with the rest of the face. Remember that ears continue to grow and will naturally be larger in an older person.

You can feel the ears and run your fingers around the curves to get to know them better.

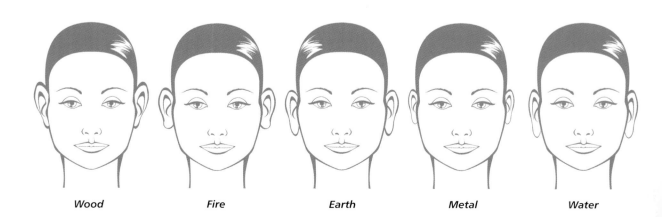

Wood   *Fire*   *Earth*   *Metal*   *Water*

WHAT TO LOOK FOR

Position Look from the front to see where the ears are set on the face. For example, the lobes could be as low as the mouth or the top as high as the eyebrows. The higher up on the head, the greater the presence of wood chi. This suggests a predominance of up energy that stirs the mind leading to greater mental activity.

The lower on the head the greater the influence of earth chi. Such a person will be more realistic and cautious while having the common sense to do the right thing when in difficulties.

Size Large ears have traditionally been a sign of good constitutional health and a long life in the Orient with the influence of water chi. These people can be risk-takers and deep down have the courage to put themselves into challenging situations. Small ears suggest the person will have a greater desire to integrate and please other

people, and have a lack of water chi. Such a person will typically be more careful with others and have a greater awareness of society's little rules.

Shape Ears that are well developed and wide in the upper portion indicate a greater energy devoted to intellectual pursuits. These people would be comfortable taking risks with their finances and investments. This represents wood and fire chi. Ears that are broader across the middle section suggest a greater emotional emphasis. This implies the person would be more secure in starting and ending relationships. This represents fire chi. If the ear is more developed in the lower part, the person may exhibit greater physical courage and bravery. Such a person would have large earlobes and generally appear to be stable and secure. This represents water chi.

Lobes A person with no earlobes will tend to be more physically cautious and less likely to take unnecessary risks or abuse his or her body. This represents a lack of water chi. A lobe that hangs down and is detached suggests a greater physical independence whereas ear lobes that are attached indicate the person is more likely to feel attached to family members or close friends for better or worse. This represents water chi.

Angle Ears that lie flat against the skull are a sign of metal chi, and that the person is open to hearing a variety of opinions, whereas ears that lie off the head and are angled forward suggest wood chi, and that the person is more focused on what he or she wants to hear.

Colour A feeling of heat in the ears or a sudden reddening suggests a rush of fire chi. In theory this would stem from the kidneys and be a sign of some kind of courage coming to the surface.

This man's smaller ears are set high on his head, suggesting a greater presence of wood chi.

Chapter 4

SUPPORTING FEATURES OF CHARACTER

The less obvious features of the face – chin, forehead, jaw, neck and philtrum (the vertical groove under the nose) – can contribute to your reading and help confirm your interpretation of the key five-element features.

Chin

Sex, conception and the reproductive organs come under the influence of this element, as do determination and survival instincts.

Oriental medicine

In traditional Oriental medicine, the chin relates to the reproductive organs. In terms of the five elements the chin reflects water chi and relates to sex and conception.

Emotion

The reproductive organs contain our most primitive energy and this is reflected in the chin. It is an almost instinctive energy that takes us through difficult times and is part of our survival resource. In more relaxed circumstances, the chin tell us about someone's will to get what he or she wants and the determination to stand up for what he or she believes in.

How to observe

Look at the chin from face on and in profile. Examine the shape and the area between the mouth and lower edge of the chin. When looking at the face the chin is the lowest part and appears to be the visual base or foundation for everything above.

Try masking off the chin and jaw with a piece of paper to see how different chins affect your impression of the whole face.

Making a reading

Observe the chin carefully and make sure you watch the chin when the person is talking to see it in motion. See if different topics of conversation induce the person to use his or her chin differently. Does he or she push the chin forwards or draw attention to it by rubbing it with his or her hands when issues of will and determination are discussed? When this occurs it suggests that the person has a greater prominence of water chi.

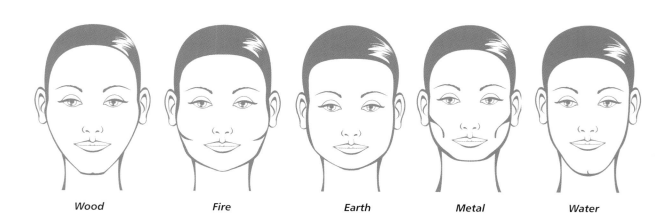

Wood   Fire   Earth   Metal   Water

WHAT TO LOOK FOR

Profile If the chin appears to recede the person may give in to other people's demands and lack the will to confront and stand up for him or herself. This person will often compensate by developing excellent social skills and charm. This represents metal chi. A strong protruding chin suggests a strong will; this person will feel comfortable imposing his or her will on others. If this is combined with a feeling of security, then such a person is less likely to engage in unnecessary conflicts. This represents water chi. A more upturned chin is associated with being more direct and stubborn. It is easy to know what such a person is looking for and there is less risk of misunderstanding, but it can be difficult to negotiate or reach a compromise. This represents wood chi.

Shape face on A square chin can emphasize a downwards earth feeling and such a person will be practical, functional and matter-of-fact. In extremes such a person could seem brusque. A round chin, which could be part of a sensitive oval-shaped face, suggests a more diplomatic approach and a greater desire to achieve his or her aims through mutual agreement. This represents earth chi. A more pointed-shaped chin is a sign of fire energy and suggests the person expresses him or herself more strongly but may be indirect in terms of communicating what he or she really wants.

Indentation or cleft A horizontal line across the chin or indentation indicates the person may have a strong will that is hard to

disguise if this is part of a strong chin and jaw line. Such a person is likely to verbalize his or her demands when others would hold back. This could mean a lack of water chi or an excess of wood chi if horizontal.

In motion Watch the chin when the person is talking to see how the chin moves. A slack chin indicates a lack of will but greater flexibility whilst a more clenched, controlled movement indicates a restrained desire to act. A slack chin indicates deficient water chi, while a flexible chin shows an excess of water chi. A clenched chin indicates metal chi.

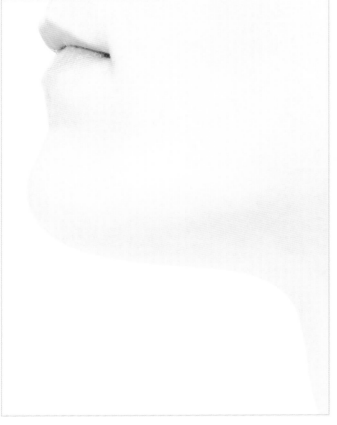

Here the chin is strong and prominent suggesting that this person is confrontational and able to assert his will when challenged.

Forehead

Three distinct regions of the forehead rule separate concerns – spirituality, reasoning and logic, and how the mind deals with practical issues.

Oriental medicine

In traditional Oriental medicine, the forehead relates to the bladder. In terms of the five elements, the forehead reflects water chi and relates to the flow of water in the body.

Emotion

From an emotional perspective the forehead tells us more about our mind and also how we use it. The chi here represents our intellect and is divided into three areas: the top represents how we use our mind in terms of spirituality, imagination, creativity and intuition; the middle shows our powers of reasoning, logic and understanding; and the lower part, close to the eyebrows, reflects the way we use our mind for practical issues. This could include planning, sorting, organizing and working through a 'to do' list.

How to observe

Look at the forehead from face on and in profile. Observe the height and width when looking face on. Ask the person to hold the hair back so you can see the entire forehead. Try not to let the hairline confuse your reading. When looking at the forehead in profile observe the angle of the forehead. Does it rise straight up or slope back, or curve back in the upper section?

Watch to see how his or her forehead moves and if it is used to make expressions. Note if the lines appear during the conversation.

Making a reading

Watch the forehead and make your reading using the information above. Carefully probe your subject with questions to see if you can verify the various aspects of your reading.

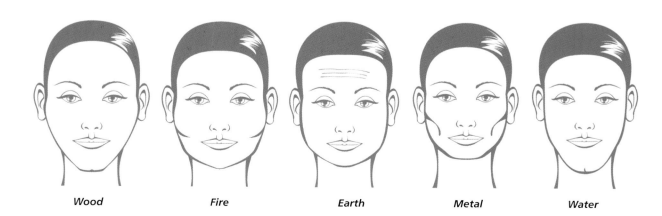

Wood   Fire   Earth   Metal   Water

WHAT TO LOOK FOR

Profile If the forehead appears vertical it indicates the person has greater intellectual independence and is happy working on his or her own. Such a person will find it easy to generate ideas and does not need the agreement or approval of others. He or she knows if it is a good idea. Water chi is present here. A forehead that slopes back suggests that the person has a quick mind and enjoys bouncing ideas around with other people. This person will find it easy to keep up with a fast-moving conversation and in extremes will be ahead of it. For such a person interaction helps stimulate the mind to create new ideas and aids in the refinement of existing thoughts. Anyone with a sloping forehead will often succeed best in a team environment. This is evidence of fire chi.

Shape face on A tall forehead, especially if close to vertical, suggests an abundance of wood chi. Such a person will often enjoy intellectual pursuits and challenges. He or she may be happiest in an academic environment. A shorter, wider forehead would indicate a greater presence of earth chi. This person will tend to be better at learning through real life. He or she may appear more streetwise and be better at making the most of the full range of options available to overcome challenges. Such a person could be effective in finding help or creating a team to overcome any individual shortcomings.

Horizontal lines
Strong lines running across the forehead come about through raising the eyebrows and can therefore be associated with a stronger flow of wood chi. This could be the result of an interest in life or due to feelings of impatience. To test ask your subject to raise his or her eyebrows. In most cases line will appear across the forehead. See if they go away when relaxed or if you can still see the evidence of lines.

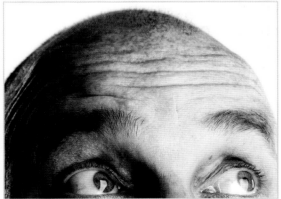

The forehead in the upper picture rises vertically but then slopes back sharply indicating a person who thinks independently. The forehead in the lower picture slopes back quickly indicating that he finds other people highly stimulating.

Jaw

The jaw reveals whether an individual is stubborn, wilful and tenacious or yielding, compliant and flexible.

Oriental medicine

In traditional Oriental medicine, the jaw relates to the liver and gallbladder. In terms of the five elements the jaw reflects wood chi and the roots of the face. This is the base from which the energy moves up.

Emotion

From an emotional perspective the jaw describes the strength of the roots of the face. This tells us more about whether the person will dig in and fight for his or her beliefs and values or take a more yielding, flexible approach.

The jaw is mobile and can be used to express emotions. A clenched, jutting jaw will create an aggressive appearance.

How to observe

Look at the jaw from face on and compare to the rest of the face. Observe the width and compare to the cheekbones and temples. A strong jaw will match these features in terms of width. Check to see how the person's jaw contributes to his or her overall face shape. A strong jaw will create a more square-shaped appearance. A narrow jaw can make the face appear more oval and taller.

Making a reading

Look at the jaw while the person is relaxed and then make a careful observation while your subject is talking. See if he or she lets the jaw drop or holds it clenched tight.

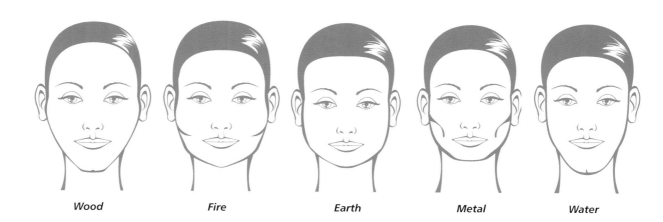

Wood   *Fire*   *Earth*   *Metal*   *Water*

WHAT TO LOOK FOR

Shape face on A wide, strong jaw line spreading out from the chin and forming the widest part of the face below the ears indicates wood chi, and a strong-willed person who finds it easy to stand up for him or herself. Such a person may relish confrontations and not shy away from following whatever he or she believes is right. If the jaw spreads across almost horizontally the person may have a stronger desire to feel in control of his or her life. A narrow jaw that appears to form more of a V-shape suggests water chi, and the person is able to adapt and still get his or her way without a confrontation. Such a person may have developed greater powers of persuasion and be able to work more patiently at swinging others round to his or her view.

Clenched A jaw that appears clenched or tight when the subject is talking is a sign of repressed emotions. As wood chi can relate to anger it is likely that the person is holding back from expressing something that brings up feelings of anger. Similarly, the grinding of teeth at night in an adult can highlight tension and a build-up of frustration that has not been resolved. Although the jaw relates to wood chi, the holding of the jaw in this way indicates an excess of inward-moving metal chi suppressing the upward flow of wood energy.

Loose A jaw that appears loose or slack when talking and perhaps falls down encouraging the mouth to open suggests a weakness in terms of the person's roots. Such a person may find it hard not to change opinions easily according other people's views and appear weak willed. This situation may be exasperated by an excess of water chi where too much water energy can lead to a looseness, dispersing any clear or strong direction.

The upper picture shows a slightly clenched, broad, strong jaw, illustrating strong wood chi but an excess of metal energy. The lower picture shows a relaxed jaw, mixing the wood chi of the jaw line with earth energy.

Neck

The neck represents the communication link between the emotions and the intellect. It is where we express ourselves verbally.

Oriental medicine

In traditional Oriental medicine, the neck connects the chi of the body and mind and has the distinction of being the centre of our verbal communication. In terms of the five elements the neck reflects wood energy as the chi of the body rises up through a person's neck.

Emotion

The neck relates to the ability to communicate emotions and thoughts and is the energetic meeting point between our emotions and intellect. It is the place where we can release emotion, warn of danger and cry for help.

How to observe

Look at the neck and consider the width and length. Does your subject have a tall, flexible-looking neck or is it shorter and more sturdy? Compare the width of the neck to the head. A thick neck could be as wide as the head whereas a thin neck might as wide as the outer edges of the eyes.

Making a reading

Look at the neck and compare with the face. Watch the person carefully while in motion, turning his or her head, perhaps tilting to one side or stretching to get a feel for how flexible and strong the link is between the heart and mind.

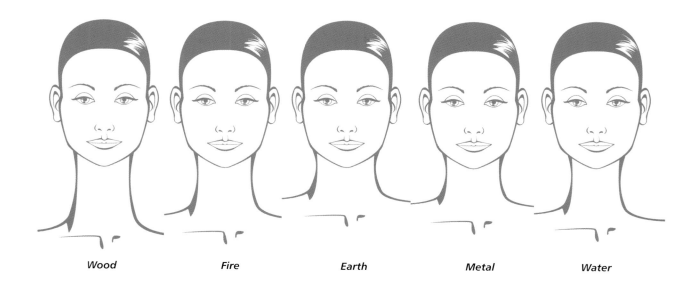

Wood   *Fire*   *Earth*   *Metal*   *Water*

WHAT TO LOOK FOR

Shape The neck and jaw tend to match each other so a thick neck is usually accompanied by a strong, wide jaw. You could think of the neck as an extension of the jaw. The neck will emphasize the face shape, and again, tend to match. For example, an oval face will often sit on top of a long neck whereas a round or square-shaped face will connect to a shorter, thicker neck.

A long, thin neck indicates a greater flow of wood chi and suggests the person is more creative, imaginative and sensitive. In comparison, a shorter, thick neck is a sign of more earth chi and therefore a more earthy, practical nature.

These shapes of neck can provide clues as to how the subject will communicate. A person with a taller neck may have a higher pitch, greater modulation and talk more quickly. Someone with a thicker neck will tend to have a lower voice with a more powerful delivery. If there is a greater presence of earth chi the person will want to choose his or her words more carefully.

A long neck that appears flexible in motion indicates an elastic relationship between the heart and mind where the person can play with different thoughts and emotions, possibly mixing up certain emotional feelings with particular ideas and then rearranging them. This person can appear less emotionally attached to any of his or thoughts. Water chi is indicated here.

A thicker, shorter neck suggests a strong link between the heart and mind. There may be more powerful connections between ideas and associated emotions. Such a person may feel passionate about certain thoughts or philosophies and find it harder to detach emotions from his or her ideas. Fire chi is indicated here.

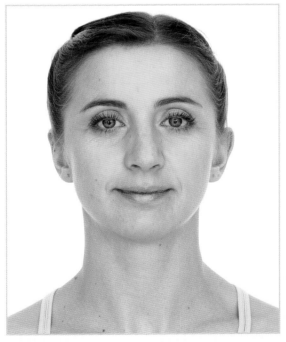

The upper picture shows a long neck suggesting increased wood chi indicating creativity. The lower picture shows a thicker earth-shaped neck suggesting a close connection between heart and mind.

Philtrum

This crease running from under the nose to the top lip is called the philtrum and represents our ability to balance and look at other perspectives.

Oriental medicine

In traditional Oriental medicine, the philtrum is associated with conception and reproduction. Indirectly, this also provides more information on the power of the kidneys in terms of chi. From a five-element perspective, the philtrum reflects water energy and is the physical link between our nose and mouth, separating the intake of air from food and liquids. The energy here is seen as a balancing point of the two. As water finds its own balance it is apt that the philtrum represents water chi.

Emotion

The philtrum is implicated in our ability to balance and see arguments or options from different perspectives. It can also indicate a readiness to change tack and try a different approach.

How to observe

Observe the distance between the upper lip and nose. Look at the strength of the valley and ridges running between the nose and mouth. View the top of the upper lip. A deep philtrum will cause the upper lip to have a strong M-shaped curve.

The philtrum will be most noticeable when the light source is from the side of the person's face and the shadows can make the philtrum look deeper than it is.

Making a reading

Look at the philtrum in relation to the whole face before looking at the detail of which five-element energy it best represents. The stronger the philtrum, deeper and more pronounced, the less it will tend to move while your subject is talking.

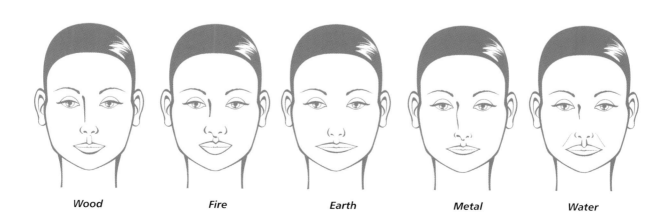

Wood   Fire   Earth   Metal   Water

WHAT TO LOOK FOR

Shape Although the philtrum represents water chi we can see each of the five elements in the philtrum and this will help further define the energy there.

• **A wood-shaped** philtrum is long and tall, particularly with strong ridges. This implies the person would be able to change his or her approach to life quickly and decisively. If something is not working he or she will be able to rapidly find another strategy.

• **A fire-shaped** philtrum is wide and open and is emphasized by pointed edges to the top of where the upper lip joins the ridges of the philtrum. Such a contour indicates a greater use of emotional energy to confront challenges and find a sense of balance. Such a person will tend to be more expressive and seek help as well as use his or her gut instinct.

• **An earth-shaped** philtrum is shorter, well developed and spread out at the lip, causing a flatter curve. This person will generally take a more cautious, common-sense approach to creating a balance in life. Any change in approach to a problem will be made more carefully and therefore slowly.

• **A metal-shaped** philtrum is shorter, with a tight narrow groove. This person may find it harder to change his or her approach when tackling a challenge and prefers to rely on persistence and inner strength to keep going. When faced with challenges such a person will retain his or her emotional balance by closing down and drawing on inner resources.

• **A water-shaped** philtrum is deep, pronounced and wide, and creates a curve in the upper lip. Such a person will find it easy to flow around challenges and explore different strategies. It will be easier to step back and see the big picture. Although he or she may feel easily out of balance or uncomfortable when faced with changes, such a person will easily settle into a more tranquil state again.

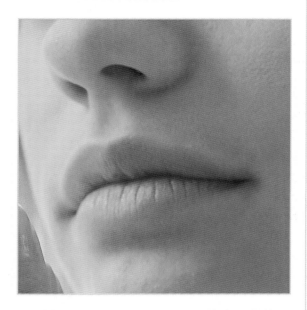

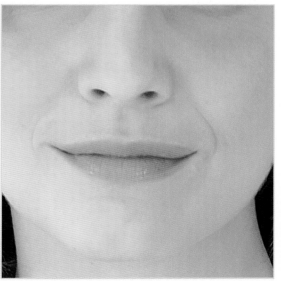

The philtrum in the top picture is wide and flared, indicating a great presence of fire chi, whilst the philtrum in the lower picture is long and narrow suggesting increased wood chi.

Liver lines

These small lines between our eyes reveal how we deal with irritations and anger and give some indication of how we get on with life.

Oriental medicine

In traditional Oriental medicine, vertical lines running up the forehead from between the eyebrows are referred to as liver lines and provide clues as to the state of the liver. From a five-element perspective liver lines display wood chi. Physically they are developed when the subject frowns, pushing the eyebrows together. This shows how energy defined by the eyebrows rises up through the centre of the face when there is tension and intensity in the flow of wood chi.

Emotion

Liver lines show how patient we are before letting our wood chi become too intense resulting in a strong upward flow. These lines are an indication of the person's impatience, irritability and anger as well as a desire to get on with life.

How to observe

Look carefully between the eyebrows when someone is in a relaxed state for evidence of liver lines. Then ask your subject to frown to see the liver lines more clearly. Look at the length and depth of the lines. The more obvious the lines are when the face is relaxed the stronger the flow of wood chi when frustrated.

Making a reading

Look at the area between the eyebrows closely and ask your subject to make a frown. Watch carefully over a period of time and while talking about potentially frustrating issues to see if the person frowns easily.

Here you can see the onset of liver lines between the eyebrows in a young person's face, indicating a tendency to feel impatient.

WHAT TO LOOK FOR

No line If there is no evidence of a liver line when the forehead is relaxed it indicates the subject can remain open and relaxed under pressure and will generally have a more laid-back attitude to life. As this area relates to our third eye it suggests the person will be interested in futuristic ideas and open to the unexplainable. Sometimes no liver line can indicate the person does not express his or her anger allowing it to turn into a form of depression.

Long single line This is a sign that the person may react quickly to stress and frustration. He or she is likely to single out one cause for any irritation and focus his or her energy on the issue more forcefully. This can be an asset when someone needs to take action quickly and precisely.

Two lines Two liver lines, usually one central line and a shorter line to one side, suggest the person is more likely to react unpredictably under pressure and may feel angry but not be able to focus it effectively. He or she may feel an element of confusion and just want to release the emotion without any practical resolution. Once released the feeling will pass quickly.

Three lines These indicate that the person is better able to disperse his or her anger and find more moderate outlets for this emotion.

Depth of line Particularly deep lines, especially when viewed while the forehead is relaxed, are a sign that the subject may repress some of his or her anger. At worst, this could lead to the build-up of some form of long-term resentment. Wood chi suppressed by strong earth chi is indicated here. More shallow lines indicate a greater ability to release any feelings of anger. In addition, these feelings are more likely to pass quickly, allowing the person to feel calm again. Wood chi is indicated.

Colour If the area around the liver lines appears to be red, the person may have a strong desire to express some form of frustration. Fire chi is indicated. A yellow colouring in the area suggests the person holds deep-seated anger and frustration.

In an older man the lines become deeper set suggesting that he has become prone to impatience and irritability.

Chapter 5

OTHER FACIAL FEATURES

In this section you will learn more about the less obvious features of the face, but features that contribute to the overall picture and can help confirm your readings of the key five-element features. As you bring these more obscure features into your face reading your interpretations will develop more depth and detail.

Lines and wrinkles

The appearance of lines and wrinkles may be an expression of experience and wisdom or of too much time spent in the sun.

Oriental medicine

In traditional Oriental medicine, the skin is associated with the lungs and intestines and they are seen as one piece of fabric. From a five-element perspective, lines and wrinkles suggest a greater presence of contracting metal chi. An excess of metal chi can lead to a look of tension in the face and over the long term will lead to the formation of lines. Lines and wrinkles are also a sign of age and therefore considered to give the impression of having experience and wisdom.

Emotion

Lines indicate a slight drying out and contraction of the skin and a few shallow lines or fresh wrinkles suggest the subject is generally feeling more detached from the details of life and perhaps withdrawing from petty issues that might once have caused emotional upsets. However, deep lines can reflect the fact that the person is more entrenched in his or her views and favours a set routine.

How to observe

Look at the skin when the face is relaxed to observe the presence of wrinkles and then make a further examination while your subject is expressing him or herself. Here any lines and wrinkles become more apparent and obvious.

Making a reading

Wrinkles and lines are a natural occurrence of age and spending time in the sun or a dry climate. You will need to assess if the lines and wrinkles are due to ingrained facial expressions. Watch your subject make different facial expressions to see how each expression influences the wrinkles. With practice you will be able to see what expression encourages which wrinkles and therefore what kind of expression these wrinkles reflect.

The lines across this man's forehead and by the sides of his mouth are shallow, whilst the lines under his left eye are deeper.

WHAT TO LOOK FOR

Laughter lines These are a result of smiling and can indicate the person is responsive in social situations, keen to please and to appear friendly. These lines could also suggest a good sense of humour and a readiness to see the funny side of situations. Fire, earth and metal elements are suggested here.

Crow's feet Lines that emanate from the outer corners of the eyes suggest a playful character that enjoys flirting and perhaps an element of teasing. Fire, earth and metal elements are suggested here.

Wrinkles around the mouth Small lines radiating out from the lips indicate a tightening of this area. This may suggest hardening of resolve in terms of work and greater focus. It could also reflect feeling stuck in life and that the person is holding on to things rather than moving forward. Metal chi is suggested here.

Wrinkles below eyes Wrinkles below the eyes when there is no swelling indicates a tightening and possible loss of fluidity. This may be the result of being more structured and feeling happier in a set routine. Metal chi is suggested here.

This is a good example of crow's feet and wrinkles below the eyes. It suggests some contraction of the kidney or reproductive organs and a dry sense of humour.

Hair

The head where the hair grows is worthy of examination in face reading and all five elements are represented.

Oriental medicine

In traditional Oriental medicine, the top of the head and the area where hair grows can be divided into different regions: the front hairline relates to the kidneys and bladder; the sides above the ears to the lungs and colon; the top to the heart, circulation and small intestines; the sides behind the ears to the spleen, pancreas and stomach; and the back to the liver and gallbladder.

Each area is also associated with one of the five elements: the front with water chi; the front sides with metal chi; the top with fire chi; the rear sides with earth chi; and the rear with wood chi.

Emotion

The way someone styles and grows his or her hair can give us more clues as to how he or she wants to be seen, and through this you can find interesting clues as to the personality. In addition, hair has its own natural qualities according to thickness, curls, colour and current health.

How to observe

Look at the hair and think about how your subject has created that particular style. Note any natural features the hair has; this can be difficult since many people artificially create waves, curls, different colour and condition in their hair.

Making a reading

After your face reading see if your subject's choice of hairstyle confirms your intitial reading.

This spiky hairstyle spreads energy out creating a flow of energy associated with fire chi.

WHAT TO LOOK FOR

Long hair This suggests the person likes the look and feel of a long mane. In a woman this is seen as being more feminine while in a man can reflect a free-thinking, spiritual being. Generally, this will accentuate the appearance of earth chi and in both sexes indicates the person is more caring.

Wavy hair We often think of naturally wavy hair as a sign of creativity and imagination. There may be some truth from a five-element perspective as wavy hair or curls suggest a greater presence of water chi. This winter, night-time chi is often seen as being ideal for original, imaginative thoughts.

Neat hair Hair that is obviously looked after and very neat reflects an orderly, meticulous mind and suggests the person has a greater presence of metal chi. This would be confirmed by regular attention to the hair and checking in the mirror.

Parted hair A parting does form an opening where our head is more exposed. Whether it is central, left or right might provide clues as to where someone wants to feel stimulated. Left would suggest greater powers of reasoning, centre more balanced and right more creative.

Short hair

Hair that sticks up can be associated with rising wood chi. It makes the person appear taller and gives the face more of an up appearance. Such a person may seem more active, alert and responsive.

Spiky hair This is associated with fire chi and was typical during the punk era. It suggests the person wants to be noticed and would like to be the centre of attention. Such a person may have a strong desire to express him or herself even if he or she does not manage to verbalize it.

This long floppy hair suggests earth chi, whilst the waves and curls give this hair a water energy appearance.

Hair over eyes Long, shaggy hair that covers the eyes creates a soft cuddly appearance that helps the person seem gentle, kind and warm. Earth chi is indicated here.

Eyelashes

These fringes to the eye accentuate the way the eye blinks and provides further clues to character. Here you can learn how sensitive someone is.

Oriental medicine

The eyelashes are associated with fire chi and tell us more about the way this energy moves through the body. In addition, blinking tells us more about the nervous system.

Emotion

Eyelashes tell us more about the way someone wants to be seen. The way the eyelashes move through blinking is a good indication of someone's current emotional state.

How to observe

It is important to assess or ask whether the eyelashes are natural. Observe the person long enough to see how often he or she blinks. Look face on and in profile to see how long the eyelashes are.

Making a reading

Watch carefully to see how the person's blink rate changes according to his or her feelings. Can he or she hold your stare without blinking? See if the person welcomes eye contact and if he or she uses the eyelashes to achieve this.

These short eyelashes indicate that the subject is down-to-earth and practical.

WHAT TO LOOK FOR

Long eyelashes Long eyelashes are associated with someone who feels more romantic and is gentle, sensitive and kind. If the eyelashes look delicate it emphasizes the sensitive side of the person's nature. They can make it easier to flirt and expose a sensual side. Fire chi is suggested here.

Wearing false eyelashes indicates that the person is trying to draw attention to the eyes and that eye contact is important to that person. Similarly, applying mascara will draw more attention to the eyes and eyelashes, making it easier to make and break eye contact.

Short eyelashes These suggest the subject is more pragmatic, realistic and logical. If combined with a slow blink rate, the person may have strong powers of

These long eyelashes can be a sign of fire chi if combined with an extrovert nature, or a water character if used to convey a more mysterious, sensual impression.

concentration and the ability to focus on details. Metal chi is indicated here.

Blink rate A faster blink rate is associated with greater water, wood and fire energies and suggests heightened alertness. In extremes, a fast blink rate could indicate fear or nervousness. Slower blink rates relate to more earth and metal chi and indicate a relaxed, contented state. Being able to hold a long stare would paradoxically suggest the person is exhibiting a more intense and focused wood chi.

Chapter 6

PUTTING IT ALL TOGETHER

Now that you have learned to examine the features of the face minutely it is time to put it all together and make real-life readings. Here you will learn more about reading a face in motion and how to recognize movements of the eyes and mouth in terms of the five elements. I have provided you with a sample face reading so that you can see how it is done and compare your reading with mine.

Five-element reading

You have looked at each part of the face in detail and learned how to read the specific features; now it is time to think about making a complete face reading.

The challenge is to be able to identify the predominant or most likely flow of chi by looking at your subject's face. If you work through a reading by observing each aspect of the face you will have 16 different pieces of information. In terms of the five elements some of these might conflict. The eyebrows might indicate the presence of strong wood chi while the mouth suggests greater earth energy or the ears may be a sign of powerful water chi. How do you resolve which kind of five-element energy is most influential in a subject?

Stand back

To make a complete reading you will need to develop the ability to step back, see the whole face and then identify those features that provide the greatest and most revealing clues as to how someone's energy might flow. From this you will have a general foundation from which to work.

Intuition

You will need to apply your intuition to successfully face read (see pages 16–17). Now that you have a better understanding of face reading in terms of the five elements you will need to develop the ability to just recognize the five elements in a face. The easiest way is to study and practise all the face-reading discussions in this book until their application becomes second nature.

This is a common theme in many activities such as martial arts, tai chi, yoga and meditation, where repetition leads to a familiarity out of which we can relax and be more intuitive. Ultimately, you would just be able to look at a face and the kind of energy flow in that person would jump out at you without any analytical thinking. This may take years to master but you can start here and keep practising.

Three most striking features

One easy way to start is to look at a face and ask yourself which feature stands out and makes the biggest impression. With one person this could be the nose, another the eyes, someone else the face shape or the mouth. Once you have identified the most noticeable feature on that person's face, think about what this says in terms of the five elements.

Now study the face to see if you can identify another prominent or strong feature that confirms a strong presence of this particular five-element chi. So, for example, you might notice the eyebrows most in one person. This indicates a strong presence of wood chi. Supporting features would be a tall forehead, long oval face, a long nose, narrow mouth or ears that are well developed in the upper portion.

If two of these support your original reading you can, for now, assume that there is a strong flow of wood chi in your subject. Should you not find any supporting features I recommend you reconsider your original reading. Was that really the most striking feature? If so, did you make the correct association in terms of which five-element chi this feature represents?

Once you know which of the five elements is predominant you are in a position to start your reading. Remember to think in terms of the times of day and seasons when applying the five elements.

Practise reading each aspect of the face and then develop the ability to stand back and look for the most important feature to orientate your reading.

Real-life readings

You are now ready to try some real-life readings on friends and family. I find it is more effective to talk through a face reading rather than make direct claims.

Begin the reading

You might begin a reading by making the subject comfortable, and making sure that you have sufficient light in which to observe the person's face. You might, after some observation, start by saying: 'The shape of your face, complexion and eyes indicate to me that you have a strong flow of fire energy. This means you have a predominance of mid-day, summer energy that can help you feel expressive, emotional and social.'

This makes it very clear that you are applying a methodology rather than making assumptions about your friend.

It suits my ethics to focus on the person's most positive characteristics and I would certainly not talk about anything that could be interpreted as negative. From a Taoist or Zen Buddhist perspective there are no good or bad energies and therefore a face reading would be free from any comments that might seem to be based on value judgements, moralistic opinions that are caught up in a particular culture and time or any attempt to persuade someone that he or she is someone with whom they do not feel comfortable.

Get relaxed

When someone asks you to read his or her face there is a tendency for the person to pose for you. He or she will sit feeling self-conscious and perhaps a little stiff. This does not help your face reading, as ideally you would want to see your subject in his or her most natural state.

Before you start your 'official' reading, have a relaxed chat; during this time you will be able to see your subject's face in motion, get a feel for which of the five-element energies is most obvious and possibly get your best intuitive insights.

Detailed observations

After this you can start to make your more detailed observations. It is now that you can look more closely, request that the hair be pulled back off the face and ask your subject to turn away so you can see him or her in profile.

This part of the face-reading interaction will hopefully confirm your initial readings and add more detail to your discoveries.

Getting it wrong

We have to be open to the idea that face reading does not tell us everything about a person and that we might misread a face. There is nothing wrong with this and therefore it is quite possible that someone will have a different opinion about his or her own character. There is nothing to feel defensive about if this happens and you may find it a great learning experience, especially if you can work backwards to find out which five-element energy your subject feels closest to and then look to see if you can recognize those traits in your friend's face.

Keep an open mind

Because there are so many variables and because face reading is dependent on the skill and experience of the reader I suggest you keep your expression during your reading open and watch what you say so that you do not sound definite or presumptuous.

As a subject face reading can be ambiguous at times – we are looking at different shades of grey rather than a black-and-white scenario. Therefore, I suggest you include words or phrases such as 'can be', 'might', 'suggests', 'indicates','is a sign of' rather than 'you are', 'always', 'you have'.

It helps to develop your communication skills to ensure that your reading is heard in the spirit in which it is intended.

Sample face reading

Now you can put everything that you have learnt together to make real-life readings. Here you will learn more in terms of reading a face in motion and how to recognize movements of the eyes and mouth in terms of the five elements. Below is a sample face reading so that you can see how I would approach the subject and compare your reading with mine.

Face shape

This woman's face shape is oval and wider across the forehead suggesting a predominance of wood energy. This indicates an alert, active mind and that she enjoys intellectual challenges.

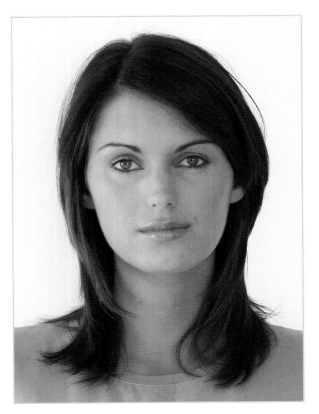

Forehead

Her forehead is broad and accentuates the appearance of an abundance of wood energy. In profile it slopes backwards indicating a more fiery mind. This fiery appearance suggests a quick mind and that she enjoys exchanging ideas with other people and working in a team. She might feel fulfilled expressing her ideas.

Eyebrows

This woman's eyebrows slope upwards indicating a strong presence of wood chi. Here we can read an ambitious nature and that she likes to move forward in life. At times she might feel impatient and irritable if other people are getting in the way of her progress.

Eyes

Our subject's eyes are close together emphasizing an inward, metal chi look to this part of her face. This shows greater powers of concentration and focus. In addition her eyes are close to the eyebrows, which accentuates the appearance of metal chi.

Her right eye is slightly larger than her left eye, indicating that she is more open and accessible in the right side of her brain. This suggests a greater openness in terms of her creative side. Her large eyes are associated with fire energy and therefore a greater desire to be expressive.

Nose

Her nose is narrow and pinched suggesting a greater presence of metal chi. This is a sign of someone who enjoys working in a team and tends to focus her emotions on one or two people or issues in life.

Cheeks

Our subject's cheeks are not full, implying an increase of metal energy. She will only feel comfortable communicating her deepest feelings with someone she can trust.

Lips

Her lips are full indicating a greater presence of fire chi. She appears to enjoy sensual experiences and be generally fun loving.

Philtrum

The philtrum is defined and represents a strong flow of water chi. This suggests that she seeks balance in life and is able to take a flexible approach to her interactions with others.

Jaw

Her jaw appears strong and well developed, suggesting a greater presence of wood chi and that she can be strong willed, working persistently and tenaciously to get what she wants in life.

Ears

Her ears are relatively small indicating a slight deficiency of water chi. The ears are high up on her head suggesting a greater presence of wood chi.

This emphasizes her intellectual and academic leanings in life.

Neck

Our subject has a long tall neck that shows an increase in wood chi and confirms a rush of upward energy through to her head. This suggests a more artistic nature and objective thinking.

Conclusion

When this is all put together we can see a predominance of wood chi. A strong presence of metal chi shows up in several areas and there are signs of water and fire chi but little evidence of earth chi.

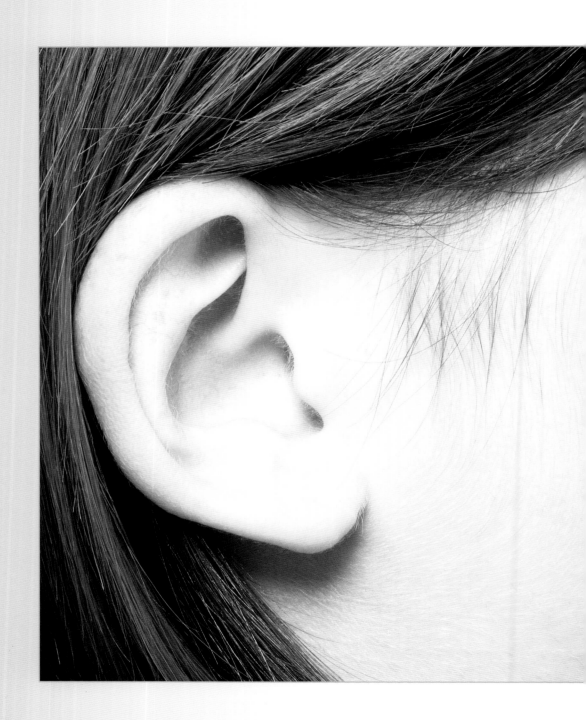

Chapter 7

FACE READING AND RELATIONSHIPS

You have now reached the point where you can apply face reading to real-life situations and test your skills. To start, we will explore face reading in terms of how you might start a relationship and then ways in which you could use face reading to help ensure the relationship works. Using the five elements we can also better understand the energy created between you and your lover.

Relationships

Five-element theory is often used to analyze and examine relationships, whether through astrology or face reading, as the energy of each element has a special relationship to the other energies.

The easiest way to think of the five elements is in terms of the times of day and seasons. Naturally, one follows on from the other, so night turns to morning, morning to mid-day, mid-day to afternoon, afternoon to evening and evening to night. Similarly, the seasons follow the same rhythm; winter to spring, spring to summer, summer to late summer, late summer to autumn and autumn to winter. So how does a predominance of one kind of energy in one person affect his or her relationship with another person, taking into account that person's strongest five-element energy?

Different not better

The most important principle to remember is that there are no good or bad combinations of energy.

They are just different. So the five elements then become an interesting way of looking at a relationship and out of it we can often get a new perspective on how better to resolve challenges between us and find greater harmony.

Three combinations

There are essentially three types of relationship:
- **Soul mate** – both people share the same five-element energy;
- **Harmonious** – the couple have energies that are next to each other in the five-element cycle such as morning and mid-day or spring and summer;
- **Opposite** – the pair have opposite energies such as night and mid-day or winter and summer.

Soul mates

Generally, when the five-element energies are the same, the couple will feel like soul mates. It is easy to understand each other and feel like each knows the other inside out. One of the risks in this type of relationship is that each will know the other too well,

This couple have similar noses, mouths, ears and chins, which suggests they would feel like soul mates.

making the relationship predictable. There is a slight risk of getting bored with each other unless both bring in elements of freshness and excitement to the relationship.

Close harmony

When two people have energies that are next to each other in the five-element cycle it is easy to feel close enough to enjoy a sense of harmony while retaining some polarity and interest in each other. Sometimes such a couple will wish for the closeness between a couple with the same five-element energy or the passion of those in a relationship of opposites.

Opposites attract

If two people have a predominance of opposite five-element energies they will find it is a case of opposites attract and can have a very exciting, dynamic relationship, making a good team as they will often compensate for each other's weaknesses. The feeling that it is hard to understand each other may detract from this at times. These relationships work best when each appreciates the differences and resists the temptation to expect the other to do things in the same way that he or she would.

These three scenarios are coloured by the actual five-element energies involved. So two people with strong fire chi may have a fiery, passionate but potentially stressful relationship while a couple who both have strong earth chi may enjoy stability, cosiness and security but feel a little bored with the

These people have different eyebrows, lips and eyes. Their female fire and male earth energies suggest a harmonious relationship.

relationship at times. The specifics of this are examined in the chart on pages 88–89.

It is fascinating from a face-reading perspective to look at a couple who have spent a long time together to see how they begin to resemble each other, and in particular, take on the same five-element look. It may be that by spending so much time sleeping, eating and doing things together that our energies merge and that over time our relationship may take on a five-element energy that we share.

RELATIONSHIP CHART

YOUR PARTNER →	Wood	Fire
↓ YOU **Wood**	Each will have an up, positive approach to life. This could be a relationship that functions well and one in which both accomplish a lot, perhaps supporting each other in their careers.	The wood person will fill the fire person with an up, enthusiastic energy and help provide greater focus, whereas the fire person will bring a more emotional, 'just do what we feel' character to the relationship.
Fire	The wood person will fill the fire person with an up, enthusiastic energy and help provide greater focus, whereas the fire person will bring a more emotional, 'just do what we feel' character to the relationship.	Each will share an emotional approach to relationships but there is the risk that if fiery arguments are allowed to dominate, the couple will find themselves separating and then enjoying passionate reconciliations.
Earth	This relationship works well if each can appreciate the other's qualities even though they are very different. The wood person may be career-orientated while the earth person is more of a homebody and wants to put more energy into the family.	The fire person will have a stimulating influence on the earth person, encouraging him or her to be spontaneous and social, while the earth person will have a calming effect on the fire person, helping him or her to find greater stability.
Metal	This combination can make for a good team with the wood chi person having a more getting-things-started kind of energy and the metal person being better at completing and resolving things. Understanding and acceptance will be important.	This relationship requires a degree of acceptance in both partners. The fire chi person can help the metal person to be expressive and social, while the metal person can show his or her partner how to develop that inner steel.
Water	A relationship between people with more of these energies can be fun and stimulating with the water person providing a powerful base for the wood chi person to be enthusiastic and lively.	This relationship would be made up of extremes and could be exciting. It certainly has the potential to take each into experiences they would never have on their own.

Earth	Metal	Water
This relationship works well if each can appreciate the other's qualities even though they are very different. The wood person may be career-orientated while the earth person is more of a homebody and wants to put more energy into the family.	This combination can make for a good team with the wood chi person having a more getting-things-started kind of energy and the metal person being better at completing and resolving things. Understanding and acceptance will be important.	A relationship between people with more of these energies can be fun and stimulating with the water person providing a powerful base for the wood chi person to be enthusiastic and lively.
The fire person will have a stimulating influence on the earth person, encouraging him or her to be spontaneous and social, while the earth person will have a calming effect on the fire person, helping him or her to find greater stability.	This relationship requires a degree of acceptance in both partners. The fire chi person can help the metal person to be expressive and social, while the metal person can show his or her partner how to develop that inner steel.	This relationship would be made up of extremes and could be exciting. It certainly has the potential to take each into experiences they would never have on their own.
Each will crave a safe, settled relationship and be home-orientated. Each should feel secure with the other, although the relationship may go through periods of stagnation and perhaps boredom.	This could be a serious relationship with the earth person bringing a more settled, practical emphasis, while the metal partner contributes a more contained strength. This is a long-lasting combination but might lack fun.	For this relationship to work well the earth person would want to be comfortable with the water person's independent nature, while the water person would want to be supportive of the earth person's desire for a secure home and family life.
This could be a serious relationship with the earth person bringing a more settled, practical emphasis, while the metal partner contributes a more contained strength. This is a long-lasting combination but might lack fun.	There is a tendency for both to feel withdrawn and perhaps be more within themselves than in the relationship; however, both have considerable inner strength and can make such a relationship work if the desire is there.	The metal person brings more consistency and permanence to the relationship, while the water person has a more happy-go-lucky, make-the-most-of-whatever-happens approach.
For this relationship to work well the earth person would want to be comfortable with the water person's independent nature, while the water person would want to be supportive of the earth person's desire for a secure home and family life.	The metal person brings more consistency and permanence to the relationship, while the water person has a more happy-go-lucky, make-the-most-of-whatever-happens approach.	In this kind of relationship both partners will be independent and feel content doing his or her own thing. It can be relationship that has a great and deep love but without anything obvious on the surface.

Dating

When dating we actively start face reading, often without even realizing it. We are constantly looking for signs that may indicate our potential lover's feelings towards us. At the same time we will be looking for clues through observing the face to see if the other person is someone we could love.

The most mobile features on the face will make the greatest impression. These will be the eyebrows, eyes and mouth. In addition, any flushing of the cheeks will provide more clues and the person may draw more attention to different parts of the face by putting his or her fingers there, for example, touching the chin will highlight water chi and sexual vitality.

Eyebrows

Raising the eyebrows is a signal of positive intent and generally gives the impression of being enthusiastic. At times, raising one eyebrow or both can appear suggestive and indicate that the person might be willing to try more intimate experiences, indicating wood chi.

Eyes

The eyes have the greatest potential for connecting with your date. This can be a playful game of connecting and breaking only to reconnect, indicating fire chi. Through the eyes a person can tease and provide clues as to how he or she might behave when in love.

The eyes are also a means to see how two people will interact. Knowing how long to hold a stare, how to break

Touching the earlobe draws attention to an area that is associated with sexual vitality.

contact and when to re-establish contact successfully requires the ability to be sensitive to the other person's feelings coupled with an element of face reading.

Cheeks

The cheeks tell us much about the other person's feelings towards us. A tendency to redden suggests that our opinion of the other person matters and that we have the potential to be someone our date cares about, indicating fire and metal chi. Cheeks that blush indicate fire chi, and can suggest a state of excitement and anticipation in our date, along with a desire to express and engage on some kind of emotional level.

Mouth

The mouth is our most sensual facial feature and during a date the way someone moves his or her mouth, indicating earth chi, can tell us more about his or her desire in terms of greater intimacy.

Pouting is a well-accepted signal that someone might enjoy a kiss. Similarly, lips that are slightly parted can indicate your date is more open and prepared to give you a chance, indicating water chi. Pursed lips can be a playful way of showing disapproval but could even signify your date is pulling back from the idea of a relationship, indicating metal chi.

If the other person's lips redden during the date, he or she may be becoming more stimulated or even aroused and in the initial stage of feeling ready to take the relationship a stage further.

A big smile can be a sign of being ready to please and send out a signal of acceptance to advances. An open mouth can be a signal of openness to intimacy.

Fingertips

We can attract attention to different parts of the face by placing our fingertips there. The most obvious demonstration of this would be to place the fingertips against the lips. This can be taken as being suggestive of some kind of sensual desire when matched with the appropriate lip movement, indicating water chi.

Playing with the earlobes can suggest the person is drawing attention to his or her five-element water chi, which in a dating context could be interpreted as sexual vitality. Placing the hands and fingers over the cheeks can be a sign of increased inward metal suggesting that your attention is welcome.

Understanding your lover

Face reading and the five elements make for a wonderful way to better understand your lover. This is particularly helpful in terms of the things that are unsaid and can perhaps help us feel less confused about the whole relationship. The guide below can help you take the lead and move out of difficult times or even avoid upsets.

I have to stress that in this way face reading can help you improve a relationship and hopefully find ways to help your lover feel happier within the relationship. It is not productive to use any of this to make assumptions or form judgements about your lover as this is not healthy and can become an excuse for you not to make the changes within yourself that will contribute to a better relationship.

Wood lover

If you have ascertained that your lover has a predominance of wood chi, he or she will relate best to you when you can talk in terms that are well thought out and reasoned. You will find that such a partner will respond best to positive encouragement and enthusiasm. Your lover will be most helpful when his or her self-esteem and confidence is high.

Fire lover

A lover who exhibits fire chi qualities will appreciate you communicating from your heart and expressing your

The mutual desire to be physically close indicates the presence of earth and metal chi within this couple.

A couple with strong water chi will have a deep and meaningful relationship, but they will also enjoy periods of solitude.

Earth lover

If you are in love with someone with strong earth chi, you will make him or her most happy by contributing to a steady, stable relationship with a strong core based around the home and family. Try to keep your ideas practical and thoughts grounded in reality. This partner will enjoy a long-term relationship in which the quality of each interaction is the prime priority.

Metal lover

When in a loving relationship with someone with powerful metal chi you can elicit the best responses by appealing to his or her inner strength. By talking positively about your lover and showing the kind of respect and admiration he or she craves you will find your lover amazingly resourceful. At the same time you may have to accept that there will be times when you lover can become withdrawn and want to spend time just listening and observing what is going on.

feelings. This person will feel most passionate about a relationship in which you embrace and accept each other's emotions. Such a partner will love acts of spontaneous giving from the heart and will appreciate and respond to someone who indulges him or her in impetuous desires.

Water lover

A loving relationship with someone who has a strong flow of water chi will thrive best if there are enough moments where you engage in deep and meaningful interactions. You may have to curb any superficial communication and resist the temptation to talk for the sake of it. Such a relationship will be strong when you can both explore subjects or your own feelings with depth.

Flirting

Flirting is our version of the mating call. Where other species might use song, colour or movement we tend to rely on flirting. Most flirting will take place through facial expression, although words, touching and dance can also be flirtatious. It is interesting to think that through millions of years of our evolution we have honed our flirting skills to ensure that we have a suitable mate with whom to produce children. Flirting is ingrained in our DNA and our faces become key components of successful flirting.

I could argue that it is not how beautiful your face is but how you use it to flirt that will be most powerful in terms of attracting potential lovers. Although most of us know how to say the right things, our faces may express more honest characteristics of the person inside. We often trust a face more than what he or she might say. This is important if that person is someone with whom we might want to share a lifetime.

When flirting, you express the real you and emphasize what you consider to be your most endearing characteristics. There is no point training yourself to hold a stare if you are essentially a shy person who would appreciate someone who is sensitive and patient. Here are some ways to flirt that will express yourself in terms of the five elements and make the most of your natural strength. Look at the element you feel best applies to you.

The wood flirt

Raising your eyebrows emphasizes your enthusiasm to start a relationship. Eyebrow movement could also be

Raising the eyebrows and looking up exhibits wood chi, and could be taken as encouragement to moving gently closer.

used to attract attention to your eyes and when you want to add strength to your words. Letting your eyes look up when appropriate will send out a message to your date of up, imaginative thinking. You could also use your hands to bring your potential lover's attention to your forehead.

The fire flirt

Widening your eyes when you want to make a point or connect more strongly can have a powerful effect on your date. This will send out a message that you are open to a more intimate relationship. You can also use your eyelashes to attract attention to your eyes.

Sometimes blinking very slowly can seduce someone into looking at your eyes more carefully.

The earth flirt

To express more earth energy try a warm, broad smile. This can convey acceptance and a caring nature. Looking down when appropriate will emphasize a more downward heartfelt, tactile energy. You could use your hands to emphasize your lower cheeks and draw attention to softer parts of your face.

The metal flirt

To emphasize this inward energy try holding your date's eye contact and even narrowing your eyes slightly when you want to make a strong point. Pursing your lips when appropriate will add to the feeling of more contained inner energy. You could rest your hands on your face seductively so that your fingertips highlight your cheekbones.

The water flirt

To flirt with an emphasis on water chi, try tilting your head and looking at your date from a slight angle to emphasize your flexible nature. When making eye contact look deeply into your date's soul, especially if you are talking about a subject that brings out deep feelings. You could play with your ears when you want to bring attention to your vitality.

Using the eyes to attract attention and as the focal point of flirting is a sign of fire chi and indicates a desire to feel closer emotionally.

Chapter 8

FACE READING WITH FRIENDS AND FAMILY

In this chapter you will learn how to apply face reading to all your relationships with the aim of being able to better understand those close to you and to use this information to communicate constructively and enjoy happier relationships. The idea is to use your face-reading skills to make the most of all the relationships you have and enjoy them to the full.

Babies

We can look at our journey through life in terms of the five elements. It is possible that certain five-element energies are more active during different phases of our lives regardless of which energy is generally predominant. The different phases overlap considerably and vary from one person to another; however, I think you will see a familiar pattern in the elements.

In the womb

Conception is associated with water chi and this phase extends into the first few years of life. This night-time, winter phase relates to a stage when we are still half in and half out of the spiritual world. Imagine looking at the stars on a winter's night.

Green and callow

Youth relates to wood energy, with its morning, springtime chi related to growth and development. It is a time of materialization in our life cycle and a time when we become more analytical. Think of new buds and leaves in the spring.

Grown up

Fire energy relates to adulthood, with its mid-day, summer energy describing a time when we are naturally more outgoing and social. This extends from early teenage social freedom to parenthood. Picture colourful flowers in full bloom.

Settled and fruitful

The earth chi of the afternoon and late summer describes parenthood. This settling energy implies focus on our children and those close to us. It is a time when we might put more energy into long-term relationships. The image is of fruit ripening on the vine.

Reaping what we've sown

Retirement and generally contracting our lives to what we really want is summed up by metal chi. This evening

A baby's facial features will change very quickly.

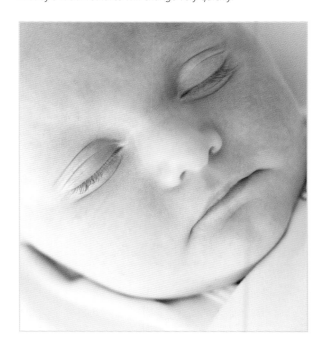

sunset, autumn energy describes a contentedness when we are more interested in what is happening inside us. The analogy would be bringing in the harvest. Finally, we move back into a water phase again and become more spiritual, moving from the material into the spiritual world.

Reading a baby's face

A baby will naturally have more water chi and it is through the ears that we can best face read a baby. You will also see plenty of wood and fire chi shown by large foreheads, big eyes and plump cheeks. Practically, it is best to use the ears, as the other facial features will tend to change dramatically over the following years.

The ears have it

Think of the ears in three layers. The top third relates to your baby's intellect, powers of reason and analysis. The middle section tells you about your baby's emotional development and ability to interact and touch others. The lower portion to the way your baby will approach practical matters and strength in adversity. In addition, the position of the ears on your baby's head will confirm the reading from the ear. If the upper ear is well developed and the whole ear is high on your baby's head he or she will have a strong desire to use and develop his or her mind. This suggests your baby will become a highly creative, imaginative and far-thinking person.

Ears that appear strong and more developed in the centre section and are more central indicate your baby

This child's ears are more developed in the upper section indicating a strong intellect.

will develop strengths in terms of social interaction and may go on to have a greater understanding of human emotions. In adulthood your child should find it easy to make friends and gain a reputation in his or her field of expertise.

If your baby's ears have strong lobes and sit lower on his or her face, the reading indicates he or she will have good common sense and a preference to be practical and realistic. In adulthood your child will be dependable and sure-footed. Typically such a person will be revered for his or her wisdom.

Children

As your baby grows into a child you might notice him or her take on more wood energy characteristics. The eyebrows will take shape, the jaw will form and the forehead will be more defined. This is natural as your child will be going through his or her growing, morning, spring phase; you will not be able to make a full face reading until your child reaches adulthood and all five elements are visible.

As your child grows you will be able to make a general reading, although it is important to remember that this is a transitional phase and you will be observing a process that slows with age.

Shape-shifting

It is normal for a younger child to have plump cheeks, fuller lips and larger eyes. These will all appear to get smaller in comparison with the rest of the face with age. The shape of the nose can change dramatically during your child's teens. Often the nose will become larger in proportion to the rest of the face representing the emergence of metal chi and the development of your child's inner strength.

To make a face reading you will need to compare your child's face to others of a similar age. Rather than be concerned about which of the five elements appears strongest, I suggest you look at the most prominent features and read those for help on bringing up your child.

Face shapes

An oval face, tall forehead, large eyes and features that appear spread out indicate that your child is more sensitive and will respond well to positive encouragement. Keeping his or her self-esteem and confidence high will help your child rise to challenges.

This child has a wide mouth, flat eyebrows and eyes set apart suggesting a strong presence of earth energy at this age.

This child will enjoy mental challenges and likes to be stimulated creatively. I would encourage such a child to fully explore his or her imagination. Water, wood and fire are indicated.

A rounder face with full cheeks, broader nose and ears that are well developed in the middle portion will suggest that your child will enjoy and flourish with strong emotional bonds. Such a child may value cuddles, hugs and tactile interaction above any verbal communication. A child with these features will cherish emotional stability and a secure family life. Fire and earth are indicated.

A squarer face with a strong jaw, larger earlobes and larger mouth are signs that your child will value time spent doing practical things with you. Playing sports, making things, playing music, getting involved in arts and crafts may be the highs of his or her life. Such a child will seek out justice and fairness. Trust

Full fiery cheeks are typical at this age when a child readily expresses his or her emotions.

and integrity will be important values in your relationship. Earth, metal and water are indicated.

Other features

A child with a large vertical forehead will often be more stubborn and happy with his or her own ideas. He or she will be good at coming up with new original ideas but if your argument does not make sense intellectually you will not find agreement. Wood chi is indicated.

A shorter, sloping forehead suggests your child will be quick and reactive. He or she will quickly work out what has to be done to get you to agree to whatever he or she wants. Such a child is often good at game-playing and will tend to do whatever it takes to get his or her own way. Fire chi is indicated.

Friends

Face reading is an amazing tool when it comes to communicating with your friends. Through face reading you can learn how to communicate to get the best response when you need to talk about something important.

Below are listed six different ways of communicating something and the kind of face that would most appreciate that type of approach:

- **Directly** – a face with metal chi
- **Sensitively** – a face with earth chi
- **Emotionally** – a face with fire chi
- **Honestly** – a face with water chi
- **Methodically** – a face with wood chi
- **Quick-wittedly** – a face with fire chi

Directly

Some people resent having the waters muddied and respect straight talking. For this person a metal approach to communication gets a better response. Few words, getting to the point quickly, and clear, unambiguous language will win this friend's respect. Such a person will typically have narrow, thin lips, eyes set closer together, smaller eyes and a more bony-looking face – all metal features. He or she will be comfortable holding your stare. This person may have eyebrows that arch up and one or two vertical lines between the eyebrows.

Sensitively

With another friend you might need to reassure, to help that person feel safe and be sensitive to his or her feelings. This interaction is representative of earth chi. Here you might prefer to be patient, slowly leading into the subject and talking in language that is gentle and kind. Such a friend would have larger eyes, eyes set further apart, fuller lips, a

Sharing a moment of humour suggests the presence of fire chi; with this energy it becomes easier to feel an emotional bond.

This person with an earth energy face would welcome a sensitive and caring friend.

interaction and suits someone with a stronger flow of fire chi.

Honestly

Some friends will place honesty and integrity above all else however painful your frankness may be. For this friend saying what you really think is most appreciated and choosing your words carefully and speaking accurately will be most valued. This friend will have an enquiring face with deep eyes. His or her eyes will have a piercing quality and seem to see right through you. The ears may be developed in the lower portion as well as having a strong jaw and chin, a characteristic of water chi.

Methodically

You may find a friend will understand you best if you explain your view logically and methodically, taking him or her through your points in a wood chi style. This person might like you to provide greater explanation for why you have reached your opinion. Such a friend will typically have a tall forehead that appears close to vertical in profile and may have vertical lines between the eyebrows.

broader mouth, cheeks that flush easily, quick eye movement and perhaps an inability to hold a stare, eyes that tend to look down and eyebrows that slope down.

Emotionally

Certain friends will look for a close emotional bond and respond much better to physical contact. Holding his or her hand, giving a hug or stroking the back may help him or her hear you better. Such a person has full cheeks, a broad nose, larger eyes, long eyebrows and ears that are well developed in the middle section. Eyes tend to look down or to the side. This is a fire chi

Quick-wittedly

A companion who is quick-witted may prefer faster repartee and enjoy bouncing ideas back and forth rather than getting stuck on any detail. For this person the art of conversation is a means of having fun and being stimulated. This type of friend will have a shorter forehead that slopes back. Such a person will have more fire chi and enjoy a fiery interaction.

Parents

When you have grown up with people and are very close to them you might find you are too close sometimes to see what your parents really want from you. The child–parent relationship is interesting as it naturally goes through three transformations. It starts with your parents being responsible for you, then changes into a more equal relationship or friendship, then evolves into a more dependent one where you are more responsible for your parents.

Because of the changing nature of the child–parent relationship it can sometimes get stuck in one phase rather then moving on naturally to the next stage. Face reading can be a helpful tool when your parents are behaving in a way you find hard to understand and when you are not sure how you can best help them accept changes in your relationship.

Can't let go of being responsible

This is most likely to affect a parent with a strong presence of earth or metal chi. Earth energy is associated with nurturing and motherhood, while metal is associated with feeling responsible and being the strong father figure. Thin lips, a broad mouth, long flat eyebrows, smaller eyes, strong cheekbones and a round or bony face shape will emphasize this.

Help the situation by introducing more water, wood or fire energy into your relationship so that you can both move forwards more easily. Water is represented by being more flexible and adaptable, wood chi by doing new things together and fire by having fun and being social. In practice this would mean taking on new pursuits that step away from any activities that you used to do together where patterns of responsibility already exist.

The father's nose indicates a fire chi that welcomes an emotional bond with his son.

Difficult to be around without silly arguments

As a parent–child relationship moves into a friendship phase, times together can be spoiled by disagreements. This is typical of too much wood and fire chi where either person reacts too quickly and says things that disrupt a happy relationship. Features that are typical in people who find themselves in this situation are: vertical lines between the eyebrows, reddish complexion, eyes that have an intense stare and move quickly.

Bringing more earth, metal or water chi into the relationship can help slow the interactions down and bring more patience and consideration into the relationship. On a practical level, try not to react, accept your parents as they are and focus on the characteristics you like the most. When you spend time together be as affectionate, loving, caring and supportive as you can.

This mother and daughter have differences; the daughter has larger features indicating fire chi, while her mother has more earth chi. This emphasizes her motherly role in the relationship.

Does not want your help

Sometimes parents can find it quite hard to accept your help when they need it. This is most typical of parents with an abundance of metal, water or wood chi. People with strong metal features may find it harder to move into a new phase of a relationship and let go, water energy people may value their independence too highly and a wood parent may think he or she knows best.

Ideally, at this stage there should be a greater presence of the nurturing, supportive, motherly earth chi to help ease into a new phase. This could mean showing greater consideration, respect, affection, understanding or patience.

Chapter 9

FACE READING AND YOUR CAREER

Learn how to apply face reading when in work situations – from job interviews to team-building exercises. Much work-related stress is created by office politics and interactions with other people; you may find that face reading helps you to step back from emotional turmoil and confrontation and see your colleagues for who they really are.

Recruitment

Although it would be unethical to judge someone by his or her face alone when interviewing that person for a job, face reading may help you ask questions that will give you better information on which to base your decision.

The secret to making this work is being able to make a rough assessment of the person's possible character using face reading and then using this to predict his or her strengths and weaknesses in terms of the requirements of a job. It is possible to say that certain types of five-element energy are better suited to certain kinds of work.

Wood energy

This energy is a more rising, focused analytical energy that is best suited to technical tasks. Examples are: engineering, design, management consultancy, software development, IT and computer services.

Fire energy

The expressive, outgoing energy associated with fire makes it ideal for jobs that require a high degree of communication skills. Examples are: marketing, sales, PR, entertainment, advertising and retail.

Earth energy

A more settled, down-to-earth, practical energy related to earth chi is best suited to jobs that require good one-to-one relationships and an understanding of human nature. Examples are: human relations, health care, social services, house building repairs and maintenance, agriculture, food services and sales.

Metal energy

Inward-moving metal energy is helpful for jobs that require accuracy, completion and tenacity. Examples are: accountancy, banking and financial services, management and administration.

Standing up to greet someone helps move energy up the body increasing wood chi.

Water energy

Flowing, water chi is excellent for work that will require creativity, imagination, flexibility, adaptability, change and objectivity. Examples are: consultancy, art, creative design, writing, photography, film, project management and publishing.

Being interviewed

When being interviewed use your facial expression to help convey the impression you think would best help you get the job. Most important is how you make eye contact. You do not want to appear evasive by avoiding eye contact so if maintaining eye contact does not feel comfortable to you, then it is worth practising on friends and people you meet when going about your daily life.

Try to focus your mind on observing interesting features about the eyes, look at the iris and study the whites of the eyes. This should help you to look into someone else's eyes for a longer period of time without feeling embarrassed. Let your interviewer lead in terms of how long you maintain eye contact.

Practise using your eyebrows to emphasize a point. Raising your eyebrows draws attention to your upper face and may signal to the interviewer that you like using your mind. Smiling is an important sign of social skills. While smiling too often can make you seem less serious and at worst, irresponsible, not smiling can mark you out as not being ready to work in a team.

Observe the interviewer's face carefully and mirror his or her facial expressions back. This can work if you feel the interviewer is looking for a like-minded person whom he or she can relate to easily. To mirror effectively follow the interviewer's facial expressions. You smile at the same time, make similar eyebrow movements and follow your interviewer's eye movements, being ready to make or break eye contact as your interviewer likes.

You can create a bond with the interviewer by mirroring his or her posture and facial expressions.

Teamwork

Using the five elements and face reading provides an interesting tool for team-working. In theory, five people working together with strength in each of the five elements would create a team that covers all areas of the spectrum.

Wood team member

This member wants to move forwards quicker than the rest of the team and is keen to take a pragmatic approach using logic and well-thought-out ideas. This person tends to be enthusiastic, assertive and active but can feel impatient and even irritable if others want to move more slowly.

Fire team member

This person will place greater emphasis on getting the atmosphere and feel of working together right. He or she enjoys the social interaction and contributes to the

In this scene, the man's face shows a cautious earth energy whilst the woman a more assertive wood chi. This can make for a balanced team as long as they can find a middle ground.

team spirit, and can help to lift the mood of the team with his or her passion for a project.

Earth team member

This member tends to be more practical and prefers to work methodically with everyone. He or she is good at making sure each member of the team is included and is considerate of others' feelings. This person may be more cautious than others and prefer to take more time and make sure everything is done correctly.

Long straight horizontal eyebrows portray earth chi suggesting a considerable team player.

Metal team member

Ideal for keeping the team together and focused on the end result, this person makes sure that tasks are completed on time and that the objectives are reached. He or she can be effective at organization and may even be the natural leader or chairperson of a team.

Water team member

Welcomed for being objective and able to think laterally, this member tends to be adaptable and able to understand and work with the various needs of the rest of the team. This person may take a more individualistic approach to work and distance him or herself from any internal politics.

Team-building

When working in a team made up of a variety of personalities, it is helpful to appreciate those differences and value them in terms of the effectiveness of the team rather than let other team members' different working styles upset you. Naturally, the team can be weighted to favour any particular assets that would help. For example, you might bring in more people with metal chi if the main aim is to sort out problems and complete the project. Alternatively, you could take the view that a group exhibiting similar five-element characteristics would find it easier to relate to each other and all pull in a similar direction.

The advantage of this is that the team will be able to surge ahead with like-minded instincts, while the risk is that they will share the same weaknesses leaving important gaps in their combined efforts.

A group of similar people working together is best suited to tasks that are clearly orientated to one type of skill or talent. For example, a group with an abundance of fire chi could put on a comedy act or a team with a strong flow of earth chi could work well on addiction therapies.

Chapter 10

FACE READING AND YOUR HEALTH

Your face can tell you a great deal about the state of your health. This can be helpful in trying to see where your health might be suffering and address the issue before it becomes a real problem. You will find positive health suggestions to go along with the face-reading diagnosis and discover more about how you can improve your health using the five-element theory.

Tip of the nose

A surprising amount of information about health and wellbeing can be gleaned from examining this small body part – shape, colour and cleft are all part of a thorough examination.

Diagnosis

It is most common to find a nose that is large at the tip becomes red more easily. In this situation there is a greater presence of fire chi and this indicates the heart is expanded and possibly overworking due to stress or anxiety. It could also be a sign that the blood is thinner. It may in some cases suggest a tendency to high blood pressure.

WHAT TO LOOK FOR

Shape Look at the tip of the nose to see if it is obviously larger than you would expect. It could be broader, bulbous or protruding. Often a nose in this kind of condition will be soft to the touch. Alternatively the tip of the nose might appear pinched and tight. In this state the nose will often feel harder.

Colour The tip of the nose can appear red, white or even purple. If you are able to observe someone in a variety of situations you will get a better idea of what his or her nose generally looks like. A snapshot reading can result in an unusual colour due to ambient temperature or recent exercise.

Cleft Sometimes the nose will have a vertical valley running down the tip known as a cleft. This most commonly will look like two vertical ridges that are set close together.

The slight cleft in this man's nose is a sign of possible heart palpitations or an irregular heartbeat.

Here the nose appears pale and slightly pinched. This indicates a stronger presence of metal chi and the risk of a tight feeling around the heart.

In more extreme circumstances the nose might appear purple under stress or after having consumed alcohol. Here the heart is thought to be strained and the blood is not being refreshed adequately. This suggests a more severe excess of fire chi.

When the nose appears white at the tip and more pinched it suggests there is too great a presence of metal chi. This indicates the heart is contracted and more likely to suffer the effects of hardening of the arteries and coronary heart disease.

A cleft suggest there is a slightly increased risk of an irregular heartbeat and possibly palpitations where the heart feels like it is racing or pounding.

What to do

The best general advice is to modify your diet to one that is most likely to keep your heart in good health. This could include replacing saturated fats from meat and dairy food with good quality mono-unsaturated oils from fish and olive oil. In addition, reduce salt and use more herbs, vinegars, lemon, lime, ginger, garlic and mustard to flavour your food.

Sugar, strong spices, coffee, alcohol and fried foods can all increase fire chi in a person and would be unhelpful for someone with a larger reddish nose. Stress will potentially worsen the situation. In this instance plenty of whole grains, vegetables and pulses would balance the excess of fire chi.

Salt and saturated fats will lead to an excess of metal chi as described by a pinched white nose. In theory repressed anger, depression or grief would make the situation worse. Salads, cooked vegetables, vegetable juices and fresh fruit will help balance the excess of metal chi.

Under the eyes

Poor health can be observed in the under eye area – colour, puffiness, creases and spots will reveal different ailments.

Diagnosis

If the area below the eye appears swollen, it is a sign of excess water chi. This could be the result of excess liquid consumption, particularly in the form of sugary drinks, colas, coffee or alcohol. Strong creases suggest the situation is more acute.

WHAT TO LOOK FOR

Shape Look to see if the skin below the eyes looks swollen. This would look like a 'U' shape extending below the eyelid. This is often referred to as bags under the eyes. Sometimes the skin here might appear swollen and sagging creating a strong crease between the bag and cheek.

Colour There is often a dark coloration below the eye close to the nose. Check whether this extends out so the whole area below the eyes has a dark or purple colour. Sometimes the skin can appear light or white in colour below the eyes. This may be due to sunbathing with sunglasses so you will need to check with the subject.

Creases There may be creases running across the bottom edge of the lower eyelid and even several creases below the eye.

Pimples
Close inspection may reveal a series of small white pimples below the eyes.

The slight pale purple hue below and in the corner of the eyes is a sign of low kidney energy.

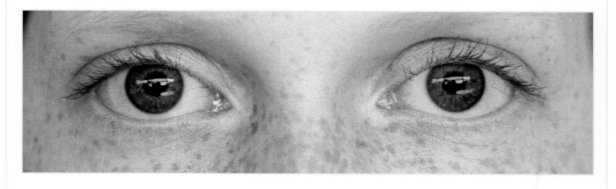

A purple colour below the eyes suggests a slight stagnation in the energy running through the kidneys, which from an Oriental medicine perspective indicates a lack of water chi resulting in decreased vitality and reduced libido.

If the area below the eyes looks flat but pale or even slightly yellow with creases, the subject may be suffering from slight dehydration over the long term and may have deposits of fat around the kidneys with a possible excess of metal chi. The presence of long-term pimples suggests there is a greater potential for clogging in the person's kidneys.

The slight swelling below the eye is an indication of excessive kidney energy.

What to do

The first step to help most issues of water chi and the energy of the kidneys is to drink the correct quantity of liquids. There is no amount that can be prescribed as our liquid consumption depends on how much liquid there is in the food we eat and how much moisture there is in the air. At the same time we can lose varying amounts according to the dryness of the air and amount we sweat.

The easiest test is to observe the colour of your urine throughout the day. The urine should appear a pale yellow. Too dark and you are not drinking enough, too clear and you are probably drinking too much.

The quality of water is important and you may find herbal teas, vegetable soups, vegetables and fruits are a good source of liquid. In addition, it is thought that alkaline-forming foods put less strain on the kidneys and here plenty of vegetables and fruit will help.

In the case of stagnant or weak kidney chi the traditional Oriental approach is to avoid any cold foods and drinks and ensure that you eat or drink hot teas, soups, stews, casseroles and porridge. Beans are considered particularly helpful in soups and stews. In addition, it is important to keep the kidneys physically warm with appropriate clothing.

To reduce the risk of fat building up around the kidneys and too much metal chi, replace saturated fats with fish and olive oils, reduce salt and include lemon, lime, radishes and shiitake mushrooms in your diet.

Cheeks

Are your cheeks sunk or full, reddish or pale, spotty or sallow? Each sign can be an indication of an underlying health problem.

Diagnosis

If the cheeks appear sunken and grey it suggests too great a presence of metal chi resulting in tightness of the chest and difficulty in expanding the lungs fully, possibly resulting in a shortness of breath. This could lead to feeling tired and depressed at times.

Pale cheeks can be a sign of a lack of fire chi and as a result a lack of energy and circulation in the lungs. In

WHAT TO LOOK FOR

Shape See if the cheeks appear full or sunken. You may need to look at the cheeks from different angles to see this clearly. If the cheeks are sunken you should notice the upper cheekbones. Full cheeks will feel softer.

Colour Look carefully to see if there is a typical long-term colour to the cheeks. They may be reddish, pale or slightly grey.

Pimples Examine the cheeks closely for signs of pimples or spots. These would not be from skin disorders like acne, acne rosacea or a rash. These would look like subtle white or small red dots on the surface of the skin.

Here the overall complexion is pale with cheeks that are sunken in the centre. This indicates a tendency to tight, weak lungs.

five-element theory such a person would be at greater risk to respiratory infections and persistent coughs. Full red cheeks indicate strong lungs with good circulation; however, if there are small white patches or pimples within the redness there could be an excess of mucus within the lungs.

White pimples on sunken grey cheeks suggest there may be fat deposits in or around the chest. Red spots suggest increased activity and that possibly the person is fighting off some kind of infection.

What to do

To help any lung condition that results from too much metal chi we can introduce more wood and sometimes fire chi. In terms of food this means eating green vegetables and particularly any that grow up strongly like kale and spring greens. It is sometimes thought that food with a shape that resembles the organ will have a similar flow of chi so here broccoli and cauliflower would be interesting choices.

Well-formed rosy cheeks indicate that this woman has a strong flow of fire chi and would find it easy to express herself.

Any fiery over-activity in the lungs like a persistent cough would benefit from the more settled earth chi of root vegetable soups, stews and casseroles. Including soaked whole grains like barley or dried beans, which have more metal and water chi, could further help this.

To break up mucus, any kind of vibration that finds its way into the lungs will help. This could be from singing or chanting. A more extreme version would be to pound your chest with soft fists while make a strong 'ahhhh' sound. This could also help the blood circulate through the lungs improving your respiration in terms of absorbing oxygen.

In Oriental medicine the lungs, intestines and skin are seen as one piece of fabric so healthy intestines and skin can help the condition of the lungs. Try a high-fibre diet with plenty of vegetables, fruit, beans and whole grains to ensure a daily bowel movement and scrub the skin of your body (not face) to help your skin breathe. Massage, exercise and good-quality soaps, oils and cosmetics will help further.

Lips

The colour, shape and movement of your lips and how the mouth is held can reveal something about the individual's state of health.

Diagnosis

Thin lips suggest tight intestines and a greater presence of metal chi. This could be confirmed if the person also has a tendency to purse the lips. Such a person may be more susceptible to indigestion.

If the lips look dark or purple there is an excess of earth chi and the liver function may be sluggish risking a build-up of toxins. In this case the mouth may look

WHAT TO LOOK FOR

Shape Look to see if the lips appear thin and narrow or full and shapely. Lips will change shape easily so make sure your subject is relaxed with the lips slightly parted to make a consistent reading.

Colour Observe the colour of the lips and note whether they are red, pink or pale. Look closely to see if there are any small white patches and whether there are any dark or purple patches.

Lines Look to see if there are a series of fine lines running away from the lips on the skin surrounding the mouth.

Movement Observe the mouth in motion. Do the lips appear pursed? Does your subject leave his or her mouth open? Does the mouth appear lazy?

Large lips and an open mouth suggest a lack of metal chi and a weakness in the intestines.

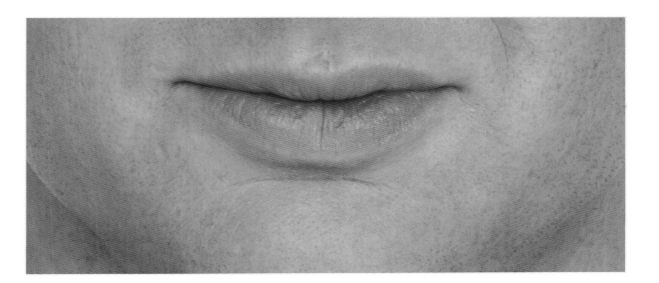

lazy when the person is eating or talking. This is most typical if the person eats a lot of saturated fats and salts as the fats can take two weeks to get though the colon. You can test this by swallowing whole kernels from sweetcorn, making a note of the time then seeing how long it takes for them to appear in your stools. Two days is ideal.

Large lips indicate a weaker intestine with a lack of metal chi and too much water chi. Leaving the mouth open would suggest this is more of an issue. Such a person may be prone to bloating and wind. If there are also white patches there may be an accumulation of mucus or fats in the intestines.

Lines around the mouth indicate the colon is contracted with an excess of metal chi that can lead to constipation.

What to do

For tight, contracted, slow or sluggish intestines a diet that is high in fibre and low in salty or fatty foods will help. Eating plenty of vegetables, fruits, whole grains

Pale lips indicate poor blood circulation in the digestive system potentially heading to poor assimilation of nutrients.

and pulses with less meat, dairy foods, eggs and salt will help. In addition, a high-fibre diet is thought to clean out the lining of the intestines and help eliminate fats that might be attached to lining.

For weak intestines a high-fibre diet can encourage the peristaltic action in the colon, strengthening it and making it easier to move the food through the colon, reducing the risk of letting toxins build up. This will also help reduce the incidence of constipation.

Again, using the 'one piece of fabric' theory (see page 119), it can help to scrub the skin of your body and carry out deep breathing exercises with chanting. Sitting down to eat, relaxing, taking your time and chewing well will all aid the digestive process and in time improve the overall condition of the intestines.

Eating your meals at the same time every day can lead to regular bowel movements and better digestion as your body knows when to prepare for each meal.

Chin

The chin's colour and the clarity of the skin are of importance when making judgements about health based on the five-element theory.

Diagnosis

A chin that exhibits a deep hollow indicates there is less water chi and therefore less vitality in the reproductive organs. Such a person may prefer to pace him or herself in terms of sex and in general enjoy more time to regenerate after periods of exertion.

Dark or green shading around the mouth suggests that there is some stagnation in the water chi of the reproductive organs. This could result in issues concerning menstruation, conception and sexual desire in women and the condition of sperm and sexual vitality in men.

WHAT TO LOOK FOR

Shape See if the chin has a hollow between the mouth and lower edge of the bone. Look at the chin in profile to see if it juts out or recedes.

Colour Look carefully for a subtle shadow around the mouth and/or across the chin. This could have a greenish shade. Also check whether the skin across the chin has a grey or reddish colour.

Pimples Look to see if there are any small pimples set into the skin. These could be either red or white and be a long-term presence.

Condition of the skin Note if the skin has an oily condition or looks greasy.

Small red pimples suggest a condition that could eventually affect the reproductive organs.

Small white pimples would indicate that there is more mucus and possibly fat in or around the reproductive organs. This might also lead to excess discharge in females. Red pimples can suggest over-activity and possibly an acid condition in the reproductive organs. This might increase the risk of bladder infections or thrush in females.

Oily skin indicates a build-up of mucus and fats in the reproductive organs. In the long term this could adversely affect the prostate.

What to do

Try to eat good-quality oils. Try to consume oils (such as olive oil) in a raw state as many vegetable oils, especially those high in polyunsaturated oil, break down when heated introducing potentially harmful free radicals to the body. Reduce fried foods.

Ensure a good supply of fresh, clean, healthy water. In general, avoid iced drinks and include herbal teas daily as cold liquids restrict the flow of water chi. The Japanese use a homemade miso soup to strengthen water chi and this is considered helpful for our reproductive organs since it is alkaline-forming and high in useful minerals.

An alkaline-forming diet may improve the general health of female reproductive organs in terms of resistance to infection. To achieve this make sure half your diet is made up of vegetables and some fresh fruit. To reduce fats and mucus include lemons, limes, radishes, mooli, shiitake mushrooms, green tea, sea vegetables, root ginger, vinegars and garlic in your fresh diet.

Primitive foods are considered to be high in the primal energy of reproduction and therefore helpful in strengthening the chi of these organs. These foods would include sea vegetables, shellfish and naturally

A beard can stimulate the water chi of the chin and result in increased sexual desire.

fermented foods all of which can be combined in miso soup for a particularly healthy dish.

Men should consider wearing appropriate underwear that allows the testicles to hang if it is necessary to reduce their temperature. Women can consider using natural organic sanitary towels rather than tampons that might interfere with the internal environment of the vagina.

Ears

Size, shape, type of earlobes and where the ears are positioned on the head are of note when examining the ears in relation to health.

Diagnosis

Larger ears are considered to indicate a strong constitution in Oriental medicine. This suggests strong water chi providing the energy for regeneration, self-healing and vitality. This effect is accentuated if the person has large, detached earlobes.

Smaller ears and earlobes that are attached are a sign that the person would benefit from looking after his or her kidneys and making the most of the available chi. In Eastern thinking this can mean the person with the smaller ears outlives the person with the larger ears as he or she will adopt a healthier

WHAT TO LOOK FOR

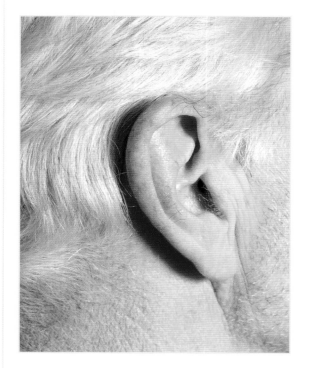

Shape Look at the size of the ear in relation to the head and make note of the shape of the ears. Are they more developed at the top, middle or bottom?

Earlobes Examine the earlobes to note their size in relation to the whole ear and see whether they are attached. Look at the lobe carefully to see if there is a deep diagonal crease running across the lobe pointing to the eyebrows.

This man has a well formed detached earlobe. The ears and lobes grow with age so in an older person this ear is not large.

lifestyle and take less risks than the person with larger ears who may become complacent and abuse his or her health.

Ears that appear well developed in the upper third suggest that the heart and lungs benefit from a healthy flow of chi. Appearing well developed in the centre third suggests a strong presence of chi in the liver, stomach, spleen and pancreas, while ears that are well developed in the lower third reflect a greater movement of chi in the intestines, kidneys, bladder and the reproductive organs.

A diagonal crease on the lobes pointing up to the eyebrows suggests an increased risk of coronary heart disease. This break in the midnight water chi can adversely influence the balance with mid-day fire chi associated with the heart.

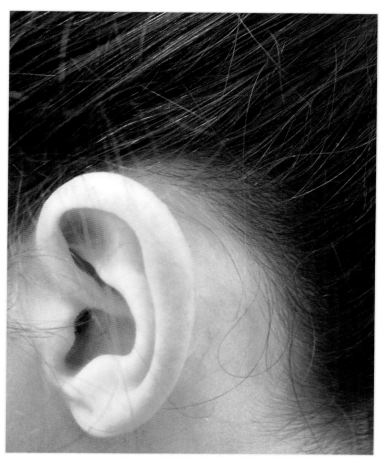

What to do

If the ears are small, enjoy everything in moderation. Regular binge-eating, drinking or drug-taking could be more risky and have a negative impact later in life. One of the benefits of this condition is that there is greater awareness of natural limitations, making it easier to respect self-imposed boundaries. Again, liquids are important for the quality of water chi and all the advice given for under the eyes (see pages 116–117) and the chin (see pages 122–123) would also apply. In addition, aduki beans are considered helpful for the energy of the kidneys. These can be used in soups, stews or cooked with grains.

These smaller ears are well developed in the upper section suggesting a stronger heart and lungs.

Try not to get run down, overly exhausted, highly stressed or get into extremely unhealthy situations as the recovery time could be longer. It is important at times of low energy to keep the kidneys warm. In Japan one remedy to restore the water chi of the kidneys is to place a hot damp towel soaked in hot ginger water across the lower back repeatedly for about 10 minutes until the area feels hot. Good sleep will also be desirable.

Whites of the eyes

Whether using Oriental medicine or more conventional Western medicine, the whiteness of the eyes is seen as a marker of health.

Diagnosis

A blue tint to the whites of the eyes indicates long-term exposure to cooling energy. This could be from cooling foods such as ice cream, sugary foods or soft drinks. This would indicate a lack of fire chi and could result in a weak immune system, feeling cold or lacking energy.

A yellow hue to the whites of the eyes suggests that there is a build-up of fats around the middle organs and that the liver has been overworked. This is a sign of a deficiency of wood chi and may precede problems in digesting fats, an increased risk of gallstones or high cholesterol.

WHAT TO LOOK FOR

Colour Examine the whites of the eyes to see the particular hue of white. The white of the eye might have a blue tint or yellow hue. The eyes could also be bloodshot. If so, you would want to find out if there is a reason for this such as an infection or the wearing of contact lenses.

Patches Look carefully at the eyes to see if you notice any small yellow, brown or dark patches. Note their position within the eye.

A blue tint is a sign of a colder energy that could lead to feeling weaker in the long term.

Yellow, brown or dark spots in the whites of the eyes suggest that the chi in certain organs could be stagnant or congested. This could be due to poor blood circulation in that part of the body and may be due to an accumulation of fats.

Marks above the iris relate to upper organs, including the brain, lungs and heart. Marks to either side of the iris suggest the middle organs of the liver, stomach, spleen or pancreas are affected, while marks below the iris indicate that the lower organs such as the intestines, reproductive organs, kidneys, bladder are affected.

What to do

For a situation where the whites of the eyes appear slightly blue, avoid cold foods such as iced drinks, ice cream and frozen foods. Be careful of sugary foods and drinking too much water. Take more hot herbal teas, cooked foods, use fresh root ginger and garlic, try mild spices and round vegetables such as onions, pumpkin, swede, turnips or cabbage to take in more fire chi.

A slight blue tint to the whites of the eyes suggests an internal coldness that could affect the water energy of the kidneys.

When the eyes appear yellow increase the absorption of wood chi by eating more leafy green vegetables, salads, pickles, lemon, lime, radishes, mooli, barley and green tea while reducing foods high in saturated fats and oils.

If the marks suggest stagnation in the upper organs eat more leafy green vegetables such as kale, watercress, parsley, spring greens, leeks and Chinese cabbage. For marks indicating stagnation in the middle organs eat more round vegetables, for example, onions, pumpkin, swede, turnips or cabbage. When marks are a sign of stagnation in the lower organs eat more root vegetables including carrots, parsnips, mooli or burdock. These could be cooked into stews, soups or casseroles.

The face in motion

Determining which features of the face move most will help you discern certain health issues and gives clues as to which element is stronger.

WHAT TO LOOK FOR

Observe the face over a period of time to see how different features move. This will be most effective if you can watch the person while he or she is experiencing a range of emotions. You might be able to precipitate this by asking questions about the past, relationships, work, childhood experiences and so on. During your face reading focus on the parts of the face that move most. The eyebrows, eyes and mouth will attract the most attention but also watch the forehead, cheeks and jaw for more subtle movements. There are five conditions you may be able to see in the face.

Excess wood chi If the face has eyebrows that move up frequently, eyes that tend to look up, a mouth that opens in a way that the lips part vertically but remain narrow, a forehead that wrinkles frequently, noticeable jaw movements and a vertical line between the eyebrows there may be an excess of wood chi.

Excess fire chi A face that looks reddish, mouth that opens wide, cheeks that puff up when smiling, eyes that flick around the room quickly and then sometimes change to an intense stare, all combine to suggest an excess of fire chi.

Excess earth chi Should the face appear to sag or droop, the ends of the mouth turn down, the eyes tend to look down frequently, the cheeks seem full at the lower part and the mouth be left open, it would suggest an excess of earth chi.

Strong liver lines between the eyebrows emphasize a strength of wood chi.

Excess metal chi When the face seems tense, tight or contracted, the lips appear pursed, jaw clenched, eyes motionless but avoiding contact and colour lifeless with a gaunt look, it is likely that there is an excess of metal chi.

Excess water chi A face with deep eyes with dark bags below, makes fluid expression changes, looks watery and has skin that seems translucent suggests excess water chi.

Diagnosis

An excess of wood chi can adversely affect the liver in the long term. It could contribute to feelings of irritability, impatience and tension.

Too much fire chi increases the risk of feeling stressed, straining the heart, high blood pressure, hypertension and panic attacks.

Increased earth chi can lead to digestive disorders, overeating, dissatisfaction with life, indecision, a susceptibility to infectious illnesses and stagnation.

Elevated levels of metal chi can contribute to feeling withdrawn, poor circulation, poor respiration, lethargy, depression and constipation.

Overly strong water chi risks frequent urination, bladder or kidney infections, reproductive problems, and feelings of fear, paranoia and insecurity, feeling physically cold and poor sleep patterns.

What to do

For food to restore the balance of each five-element energy try the following:

- To calm excessive wood chi try eating more root or ground vegetables, for example mooli or radishes, as well as sauerkraut, shiitake mushrooms, lemon and lime.
- To reduce excessive fire chi eat more vegetable-, grain- or bean-based soups; try kukicha or chamomile tea, hot apple juice and porridge.

- To counter too much earth chi eat plenty of salads, steamed green vegetables, fresh vegetable juices, peppermint tea and fruits.
- To balance an excess of metal chi try eating more spices, garlic, root ginger, berries, lightly cooked vegetables, sautéed onions, mushrooms and cucumber.
- To moderate strong water chi eat more vegetables, stews, casseroles, cooked fruits, barley, herbs and sea vegetables.

Strong emotions can sometimes be a sign of a tendency towards stress, hysteria and panic attacks, which suggests an excess of fire chi.

Chapter 11

SENSING ENERGY AROUND THE FACE

In this final chapter you will discover how to see and feel the energy around a person's head. Although this is not essential for a visual face reading it will broaden your experience and appreciation of how energy or chi moves through the body. You will also learn how to identify and use key acupressure points on the head to help change the chi there and indirectly change the way you feel.

Seeing auras

Our chi is not confined within our bodies, but surrounds our physical bodies like an envelope and is known as the aura. There is a chi energy field (or aura) around the skull in a continuation of this aura and it can be photographed using a process known as Kirilian photography. It is thought that babies and young children have the ability to see the chi around our heads and consequently often colour in a yellow halo around their drawings of people.

Practise

After some practice seeing auras you can move on to looking at the colours in this outer chi energy field. The shades of colour are subtle and you are looking for hints of a tint. Most common are yellows, greys, greens, blues and turquoise. Sometimes the aura may appear yellow close to the head but has an outer band of green.

The size, shape and colour of the aura can change quickly depending on the person's chi flow at the time and for this reason they are interesting to see but only as a snapshot of the person's energy at that time.

Once you have developed this skill you will be able to observe people's auras in a variety of situations, whether in a café, museum, train, library or anywhere people tend to be still for a while.

With practice you can see an aura around someone's head. This is easiest against a white background. Begin by looking for a light grey or silver haze around the head.

Exercise

To see someone's chi energy field you will need to have a room with a white wall and a friend with whom you can practise.

1 Ask your friend to sit about 2 m (6 feet) away from the wall and then stand yourself about 4 m (12 feet) from the wall with your friend between.

2 Try to focus your eyes about halfway between your friend and the wall. A third person could hold his or her finger here to give you something to focus on initially.

3 While you hold your focus look carefully to see if you can observe a light haze around your friend's head. It may look like a lighter coloured shadow that has been projected on to the wall behind. Sometimes it is easier to see if you sway or move your head gently so you can see the aura move against the background of the wall.

4 Try to see a light, possibly grey haze. This will usually be about 1–2 cm (½ inch) from the head. Some people's auras will appear stronger depending on their mood or energy at the time so it is worth trying with a variety of people.

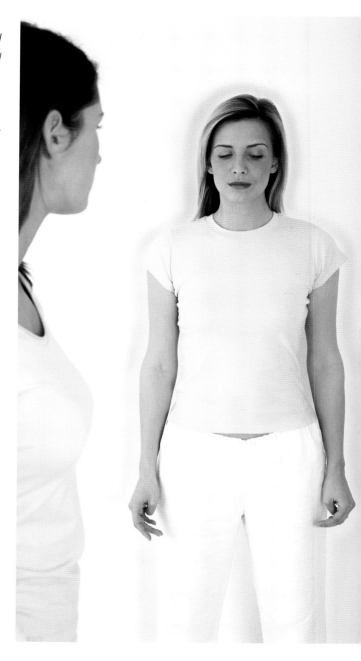

Stand about 2 m (6 feet) from a friend and then look around his or her head for a light haze against a light background.

Feeling the energy of the mind

This exercise is designed to try to develop your own sensitivity to chi – specifically other people's chi. Use it as a way to further understand the way chi energy works and how you can tune into it.

The human mind tends to use different parts of the brain to think different kinds of thoughts. If you think intensely about the future you will have more active chi in one part of your head, whereas trying to remember something will generate greater chi in another part of your skull.

The idea of this exercise is to try and feel this chi and experience it move in the head according to what the subject is thinking.

Keeping your hand about 1 cm (½ inch) from the head, move one hand slowly over it, including the forehead and back of the head.

Exercise

To do this exercise you will need a friend who is very good at focusing his or her mind. Ask your friend to sit or kneel so that his or her head is at a comfortable height for your hands.

1 Make sure you are relaxed, your hands are warm and that you are feeling mentally calm and receptive.

2 Move your hands carefully over your friend's head being particularly aware of any hot spots or areas where you feel a stronger magnetic pull as you move your hands away and towards the head. Make a mental note of areas that feel hotter.

3 Now ask your friend to think about the future or make up something in his or her imagination. For this to work it is essential that your friend does not slip into thinking about something from the past. For example, avoid thinking about where he or she would like to go on holiday next but actually accessing images of somewhere from a previous holiday or from a magazine. It might be better to imagine different shapes and colours moving around with closed eyes. It may help to let the eyes roll up slightly as though looking at the inside of the forehead.

4 Feel your friend's head again and see if you can detect any changes in the way the head feels. Once you notice some changes mark them down or memorize them.

5 Next ask your friend to try to remember an event from the past. Ask him or her to remember in great detail. This will be more effective if they struggle to remember some aspect of this, such as what they ate or who was there. Again, it will help if your friend closes his or her eyes, but this time suggest he or she looks down.

6 Once your friend is fully in this state start to move your hands around your friend's head again and look for any new hotter spots or places with a stronger magnetic pull. Remember to include the back of the head. Once you have finished your search make notes of any changes.

7 Finally, after a rest, ask your friend to clear his or her mind and then go back to one of the thought patterns he or she used before. Now feel the chi around his or her head again and see if you can work out whether your friend is imagining something new or trying to remember an event.

Acupressure

We have seven large energy centres or chakras where chi spirals and swirls. These are located at the pubic bone, navel, stomach, heart, throat, between the eyebrows and the crown of the head.

From these energy centres we have 14 pairs of meridians. These are large paths of chi. Six of these run along our limbs to our hands and feet. Along each meridian there are various points, known as *tsubos* where it is thought we can influence the flow of chi more easily.

The chakras focus the chi – particularly in terms of bringing external chi into the body and then from the chakras chi drifts off to form meridians; the many, many acupressure points throughout the body, including the head, also function as smaller transmitters of energy or tsubos. It is possible to change the chi or energy in the tsubos to fine-tune the system. Here we will look at different ways to change the chi in your head using specific tsubos or acupressure points.

Start at the corners of the eyes and eyebrows and work out along the underside of the eyebrows.

Exercise

Typically your chi will get stuck in the ridges in the bones of your skull. One way to free the energy of your mind is to physically work around all the ridges of the skull with your fingers, massaging and breathing out any stagnant chi – imagine the energy around these bones moving freely with each out-breath. This should leave you feeling lighter, freer and clearer.

Doing this on a regular basis will help prevent chi getting stuck in places where it might cause certain headaches. As you become better at working on your head you will also become more familiar with all the little dents and crevices in your skull that are helpful for locating tsubos.

1 *Begin by pushing your fingers into the ridge just above your eyebrows. Put your thumb into the lower ridge that makes up the opening to your eye socket. With your fingers and thumbs work out from the centre until your fingers reach your temples.*

2 *Use your fingers to explore the hollow in your temples. At the edges of this hollow you will find small ridges that are usually painful to push against. Work your way around your temples trying to keep chi moving. Remember to breathe your own chi out through your fingers into your head as you massage your temples.*

3 *From your temples move your fingers to your lower eye socket and work back to your nose. Rub into the crease where your nose joins your cheekbone and slowly move down until you are rubbing against the sides of your nostrils. Here you will find another small indentation. You will have to push against your nostril to find it. Press into the indentation to free your chi there.*

4 *From your nostril move your finger out horizontally until you are directly below your eye. Here you will find another indentation you can work your fingers into. After this keep going until your fingers are located in front of your ears. Now you will find a hollow where your jawbone meets your skull. You might find it easier to locate if you clench your jaw. As you relax your jaw your finger will sink further into the hollow.*

5 *From your ear you can work around your jawbone, squeezing with your fingers and thumbs until your hands meet at the front. Finally put your hands behind your head so that your thumbs are located at the base of your skull and let your fingers rest on your upper head. Starting from the centre work along the ridge at the bottom of your skull slowly moving out until you come to the back of your jaw.*

Working on the tsubos

The following tsubos or acupressure points, which are on the head, will all influence the chi of your mind. I have described how they do this, what they are good for, where to find them and how to use them.

You should work on the tsubos on both sides of the head. Using both hands, on either side of the head, generally press firmly into each point about six times.

Breathe in, press your thumb or finger into the point, breathe out and imagine you are channelling chi into the tsubo each time.

Welcome Fragrance tsubo

Use this exercise for a blocked nose and for relaxing your face.

1 *Put your fingers on either side of your nostrils, push against your cheekbones and slide your fingers very slightly towards your nose until you feel a slight hollow in the bone. This tsubo is usually quite painful.*

2 *Carefully breathe chi into the point. If you have a blocked nose, press firmly and slide your fingers horizontally outwards and round to your ears as you breathe out.*

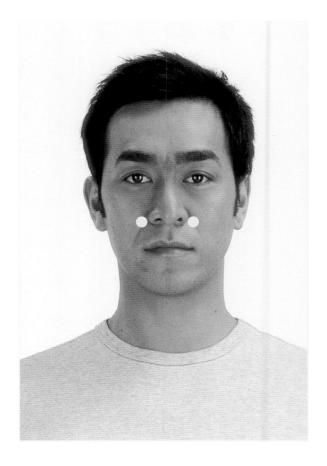

Empty Space in Bone tsubo

Use this exercise for blocked sinuses.

1 *Look in the mirror and slide your thumbs vertically down from your eyes until you locate a hollow at the bottom of your cheekbone. Your thumbs should be in line with your nostrils.*

2 *Circle your thumbs in the hollow until you find the most sensitive area. Then breathe chi into this specific point.*

Windy Pool tsubo

Use this exercise for pains at the back of head and discomfort in the eyes.

1 *Find the ridge at the base of the rear of your skull with your thumbs. Keep your hands open so that your fingers rest near the top of your head. Slide out from the centre until you cross the main tendons running under the ridge. You can feel them by tipping your head forward and then lifting it slowly. Just outside these tendons you will find two hollows in the ridge. Press into them to find the tsubo.*

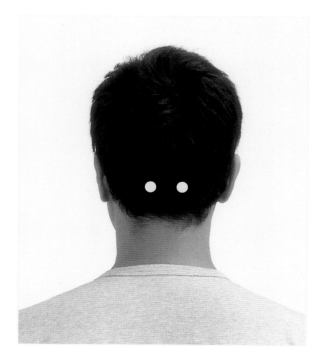

Index

About the author

Simon Brown studied Oriental medicine with Michio Kushi, Aveline Kushi and Shizuko Yamamoto. He ran complementary health centres in Philadelphia and London where he worked with many leading practitioners in the field of healing.

He began his writing career after many years of working as a practitioner in the fields of macrobiotics, Shiatsu, Feng Shui, Reiki and astrology. His first book *The Principles of Feng Shui* came out in 1996 and was followed by *Practical Feng Shui*, which sold nearly a million copies. Since then, Simon has written about macrobiotics, chi energy, Do In, Japanese astrology and face reading.

Simon is the chairperson of the Macrobiotic Association of Great Britain as well as a practitioner member of the Shiatsu Society of Great Britain and Feng Shui Society of Great Britain.

Simon Brown is available to consult on using face reading to discover what kinds of foods might best help achieve optimum health. This can be done in person or by phone and email depending on your situation. Please visit www.chienergy.co.uk for further details.

Courses

For courses and training in face reading, macrobiotics and Feng Shui please visit www.chienergy.co.uk for the latest details.

Other books

Modern Day Macrobiotics, Carroll & Brown
The Feng Shui Bible, Godsfield Press
Chi Energy Workbook, Carroll & Brown
Feng Shui in a Weekend, Hamlyn

Contact details

Simon G. Brown
Tel.: +44 (0) 20 7431 9897
E-mail: simon@chienergy.co.uk
Website: www.chienergy.co.uk

Acknowledgements

Alamy/Larry Lilac 16. BananaStock 98, 99. Corbis UK Ltd/Ajax/zefa 17; /Dex Images 21; /Glenn Weiner 35; /Grace/zefa 116; /Gregory Pace 39; /Heide Benser/Veer 104; /Jennie Woodcock; /Reflections 126; /Larry Williams/zefa 102; /Lucidio Studio inc 117; /Malcolm Hanes 127; /Mika/zefa 92; /Mitchell Gerber 31, 33; /Newmann/zefa 103; /Peter Frank/Veer 93; /Peter M. Fisher 23; /Rune Hellestad 37; /Serge Krouglikoff 72; /Simon Marcus 91; /Stefan Schuetz 49; /Tim Kiusalaas 129. Getty Images 19 top centre; /Adrian Weinbrecht 66; /B2M Productions 105; /Bruce Laurance 128; /Chabruken 20; /Dave Greenman 59 bottom right; /Lucas Lenci Photo 111; /Michael Blann 119; /Patricia De La Rosa 74; /Peter Cade 87; /Spike Mafford 78; /Stuart O'Sullivan 108; /Wang Leng 9; /Zac Macaulay 25, 124; /Zia Soleil 109. istockphoto.com 19 centre. imagesource 8, 70, 114. Octopus Publishing Group Limited 26, 81; /Frazer Cunningham 65, 82, 83; /Ian Wallace 136 139; /Jane Gilchrist 90, 95; /Mike Prior 4 bottom, 14, 15, 43, 47, 51, 53, 61 bottom right, 73, 121, 123, 138, 63 bottom right; /Russel Sadur 57 65 top right. PhotoAlto 1, 2, 6, 28, 40, 54, 68, 76, 84, 96, 106, 112, 130. PhotoDisc 27, 71, 86. Shutterstock 120; /Andriy Solovyov 61 top right; /Anna Braga 24; /Debbie Vinci 118; /Diego Cervo 94; /Elena Elisseeva 59 top right; /Frenk and Danielle Kaufmann 115; /Giorgio Gruizza 45; /Ilya Rabkin 122; /Keith McIntyre 19 centre bottom; /Lara Barrett 125; /Marilyn Barbone 75; /photobank.ch 100; /Simone van den Berg 67; /Solovieva Ekaterina Aleksandrovna 63 top right; /Yuri Arcurs 22; /Zsolt Nyulaszi 110. The Art Archive/Private Collection/Gianni Dagli Orti 11. TopFoto/Charles Walker 13.

Executive Editor Sandra Rigby
Managing Editor Clare Churly
Executive Art Editor Sally Bond
Designer Janis Utton
Illustrator Javier Joaquin
Picture Library Assistant Taura Riley
Senior Production Controller Simone Nauerth